The Soup of Life

Margaret Valone

Copyright © 2015 Margaret Valone

All rights reserved.

ISBN-10:1502574454
ISBN-13:9781502574459

Also by Margaret Valone

Keep Laughing – Suture Self

Life is Sugar and Vinegar

DEDICATION

To all my readers who encouraged me to create a book of selected favorite columns

INTRODUCTION

This is not a cookbook. It is about learning and living with humor. It is sure to appeal to young parents and grandparents alike. I have always felt that life is like soup. The more good ingredients you add to it the better it is. So, why have thin gruel when you can have a hearty stew?

When I was a child I was told that I had a rheumatic heart, a heart with a leaky valve. I could have played it safe and lived a very quiet, passive life. But I chose to live a full life. I put a lot of good stuff into my life. Good friends, exercise, sports and travel. I made the soup of my life great.

It was not until I was 52 years old that I was accurately diagnosed. It turned out that I was born with a hole in my heart. It was the size of a silver dollar. I used to say, "I was born with a hole in my heart. I put Jesus in and then they patched it up with Teflon." This was in 1976 and it is still holding.

CONTENTS

ABOUT THIS COLUMN 1

What are My Columns About? 1

Why I Write 3

All About Love 6

Always Be Kind 9

The Joy of Living 11

My Own Soap Opera 14

PHILOSOPHY AND THOUGHTS 16

How Do You Want People to Remember You? 16

IQ Versus EQ: 20

Utilize Your Strongest Assets for a Positive Outlook 20

Like a Fine Wine, Life Gets Better With Age 22

Cooking up the Soup of Life 25

Sturdy Foundations Mean Good Marriages 27

Spreading Cheer 29

WORDS AND LANGUAGE 32

Let's Talk About Words and Thoughts 32

Maximize Experience through the Mind 34

Open the Lines of Communication Gracefully 36

Positive News Is Good for the Soul 38

Showing Life's Choices through Actions 41

Reflecting on the Turning Points of Life 43

Simplify Your Life, Get Rid of the Clutter 45

Don't Be Shy With Compliments 47

Choosing Your Words Carefully 49

The Marvels of Language 52

Words Have the Power to Change Lives 55

HINTS 58

Taking Inventory of Yourself Can Be an Uplifting Experience 58

What Makes You Happy? 61

Thoughts on Nature 64

You Can Change Things, Yourself ... 66

Fighting the War on Drugs ... 69

Let's Make Our Society Better ... 73

HUMOR ... 76

Learning through Laughter ... 76

Laughs, Peppered with Some Groans ... 78

Laugh Often ... 81

Finding Laughter, Happiness and Health ... 84

Learning through Humor ... 87

Embrace Your Sense of Humor ... 90

Finding Humor in the Operating Room ... 92

A Dose of Humor ... 94

Philosophies That Tickle Your Funny Bone ... 96

The Art of Conversation ... 98

RELIGION ... 100

Introduction to Religious Holidays ... 100

Jesus Is the Reason for the Season ... 103

Merry Christmas, Everyone ... 106

Jesus Gives Us Second Chances ... 109

Celebrating the Spirit of the Season 112

Pondering the Meaning of Christmas 115

Dreaming of a White Street Christmas 117

Living in the Presence of God 119

Easter Musings 121

Keeping the Faith This Easter 124

Remembering the True Meaning of Easter 127

HOLIDAYS 129

New Year, New You 129

For the New Year, Take Some Inventory 132

Happy Father's Day 134

Sharing Your Love with Others Every Day 137

A Father's Role 139

The Changing Role of the Father 141

Gold Nuggets of Wisdom 144

Are You a Good Mother? 147

Cherish Your Loved Ones Every Day 149

Happy Mother's Day! 152

FOOD AND HEALTH 155

Putting the Perfect Spin on Pizza 155

The Secret's in the Sauce 157

Body, Mind and Spirit 159

Come On, Get Healthy 162

Weight and Health 165

Diving into Healthy Habits 167

Healthful Hints 169

How to Be Happy and Healthy 172

Life's Little Remedies 175

Live Healthier and Happier 177

Dreams, Dollars and Diets 180

Health Help 182

Hints on Gout 184

Choices and Good Health 187

Cooking up Some Fun 190

POLITICAL 192

Thinking Deeply about Government Issues 192

Character Development 194

Journalism Matters 197

Waxing Political 200

Reflecting on Our Nation's Problems 203

Sharing Your Thoughts 206

Voice Your Opinion 209

What Happened to America? 211

It's Time to Take Action 213

There Is No Such Thing as Failure 217

The Pros and Cons of Gambling 221

Defining a Gift 223

A Healthy Serving of Advice 225

Thank You All 228

ABOUT THE AUTHOR 230

ABOUT THIS COLUMN

What are My Columns About?

When people find out I write a column, they ask me, "What kind of column do you write?" I really don't know how to answer that. How would you answer that?

I'm not a "Dear Maggie". I'm not a recipe columnist, although sometimes I pass along tips to you, like this one: for Thanksgiving, I received two turkey carcasses. My sister gave me one and a good friend gave me the other. Do you ever make turkey soup with the carcasses? It's delicious and there's so much meat left on the bones! I had so many small pieces of turkey that I decided to make a turkey salad. After all, I make egg and tuna fish salads, why not turkey? It was delicious! Maybe you've done this before, but it was my first time. Now I'm telling you this because it will give you extra meals from leftovers.

Back to the subject - what is this column about? Sometimes I talk a little about politics. I really have to restrain myself on that because no matter what you do or have, it was affected by politics. For example, the cost of a loaf of bread, the clothes you wear, the kind of streets you travel on, the quality of your education, etc. That's why it's so important to get involved. Tell your representatives what you're thinking. If you don't, don't blame them when they do something different.

I like to think about philosophical things - things that are going on in our society that either affect us or we can affect them. Are you a positive person or a negative one? We do have choices. Once your eyes have been opened to this fact, your whole life can change. You have great power. You can initiate or you can react. With the first, people will react to you. With the second, you will react to them. We need this exchange.

We all have certain talents. Are you afraid to use your talents because you may appear to be boastful? Tell me, who gave you these talents? Did He tell you to hide them under a bushel? How about other people's talents that you need? I'm so dumb about computers I hate bookwork (record keeping). I'm so uncoordinated! I'm terrible with mechanical things. That's why God made men.

I love to organize, dream about potential, cook, even clean. I love people and I love to make them laugh. When I was a teenager, I was afraid to be fun, for fear the boys would think I was "fast". So, I was serious in the company of boys and not with girls. Now at my age, I can make everybody laugh.

I remembered something the other day. As I was growing up, I spoke Sicilian as well as English. Now nobody speaks Sicilian, not even the people in Sicily. Anyway, one hot summer day, I was trying to find relief from the heat. I went upstairs, laid at the foot of the bed and a nice breeze was coming in. I ran downstairs to share the good news with my mother. She looked strangely at me and said, "Do you know what you said?" She explained to me that I had said if she would go upstairs and stand on her head, she would be refreshed. So much for my Sicilian!

Why I Write

I enjoyed Dan O'Rourke's recent column on "Why Do I Write?" I write for so many of the same reasons. I too, want people to think, open their minds and see things they had overlooked. I want them to realize how much power each of us has if we are aware of all the areas in our lives and other people's lives that we can have an impact on.

There's a very big obstacle in the way. The obstacle is self. Another word that is almost synonymous is pride. If we can get those two items out of the way, we are open to all kinds of new experiences. We won't have the same experiences because we have different areas of interest. This is good because we can attract people who think like we think and all those other people can make new groups with common interests.

Sometimes you have to take the leadership and sometimes you can be a good follower. This is very important because good followers can make people of leadership successful.

I, too, agree with Dan (I can call him Dan because I used to cut his hair and no, it's not my fault that he has little left!) about teaching with humor. I used to teach my son, Rusty, spelling through association. For example, I taught him how to spell the word assume by remembering when you assume something, you make an ass out of you and me. He used to say, "Mom, I'm the only kid who laughs while we have a spelling test." If it works, so be it.

I came across an observation I had made. Remember, your brain is a storehouse. Don't make it an outhouse! There's more truth than humor in that. Think about it.

I was very impressed by the article written by Emily Fredrix. She tells the story about Nikol Hadley and how she is using her bad experiences to help teenagers make wise decisions. Now young people or old people can relate to people who have had experiences. I find this is true in my own life. I've lost a son at the age of 30, a husband, and I've had four major surgeries, two for heart and two for cancer, and I'm still enjoying life. So whenever a person is going through any of these operations, I can encourage them. I had my first heart surgery in 1978 when Cleveland Clinic patched the big hole in my heart. After that, if I found out someone was going to have open heart surgery, I would call him or her and say I was pleasantly surprised how easy it was. My varicose vein surgery was more painful. It was the truth. After I had my hysterectomy, I had my nurses and doctors in stitches and they kept saying, "You should write a book." So I took their advice and I wrote my first book. It was called "Keep Laughing - Suture Self". I made a lot of people laugh. I was in my 70s.

I came across a letter I wrote to the people's column before this column started. I wrote: "Let's take inventory. How is the U.S. growing?

1. Our food lines are growing longer.
2. The unemployment lines are growing longer.
3. The number of people without health insurance is growing bigger.
4. Our national debt is growing larger.
5. People all over the world are growing more suspicious of us daily.
6. Children in schools are growing more disrespectful because teachers cannot discipline.

Should I call these growing pains? I know they pain me." Then I said, "Is now the time to give people who have the most, more? Will they throw the money back into our country or will they take it to other countries that have cheap labor and no taxes? This will not jump-start the economy. They'll just jump ship." I thought, "Is this for real?" I could be writing this today. All these things still exist but in larger numbers.

The Soup of Life

A person on CNN said, "What would happen if the people would send back the checks in the mail and say, put it toward something like the national debt. This is because although the idea of giving money is nice, who is going to pay for it?" I thought about what he said and I thought, most people who would consider that would say, "Sure, I give my money back and nobody else does and I'm the one who's out."

So then I thought, why couldn't we have petitions with our names on it that say I will give back my check if it becomes a national movement and can make a difference?

But the real purpose is to jump-start the economy. If only we could spend it on products made in the United States only. The problem is we'd be hard pressed to find those products. The president is trying to help our situation. We have to do something. So far, both parties in Congress are not cooperating. Let's hope it's not too late.

Would you believe this week I saw eggs selling as high as $2.69 per dozen? They must be from the goose that laid the golden egg! Right?

All About Love

If you want to live a rich life, you have to get out and get involved. I'll give you an example. On Election Day, the First Baptist Church in Dunkirk is a voting place. The Christian Academy School there wanted help to sell tickets for their spaghetti dinner Sept. 25. They asked me to sit at the door from 5 to 9 p.m. I never refuse because the mother's club there is fantastic and the teachers are bright and very loving to the children. They work for love, not money. It pays off in other ways. Anyway, I learned something beautiful there. The new woman custodian came and sat with me. We've become good friends because she is so talented and I often need her help. I saw a new side of her. She was telling me about a kindergarten boy who was always yelling and disturbing the class. A monitor in charge couldn't control him. My friend, Cindy, said she knew how to get him in line.

She went up to the boy, got down to his level, eye to eye and asked, "Do you know why you're in time-out?"

"No", he responded.

"I want you to keep quiet and listen," she said. He did. "What do you hear?" she asked.

"Nothing", he said.

"That's right. The children are playing quietly. They can't do that when you're yelling. Now do you think you can be quiet like that so I can take you out of time-out?"

The Soup of Life

He nodded and was released. He played quietly. What a smart woman. First of all she gave him her undivided attention. She got down to his level. She wasn't looking down on him. They communicated. How beautiful!

Later I picked up a magazine and found an article entitled, *"25 Things Children Need."* Perfect. I couldn't have planned it better. Here goes:

1. Unconditional love
2. Healthful balanced meals
3. Regular adequate sleep
4. Frequent (daily) exercise
5. The freedom to be creative
6. Time to interact with their peers and friends
7. Hugs, kisses, shoulder rubs, snuggles and other nonverbal expressions of love from people who have their permission
8. Consistent, appropriate discipline
9. To be listened to and heard
10. To laugh
11. To feel important
12. Responsibilities appropriate to their age and development levels
13. Balance in their life
14. To be talked to, not talked down to
15. To feel valued
16. To make mistakes, to be taught how to learn from their mistakes
17. To be treated with courtesy and respect
18. To be safe
19. To have their feelings validated and affirmed
20. Consistent predictable limits
21. Honesty and truth
22. To be taught what they don't know
23. To be flexible
24. Physical and mental relaxation
25. Intellectual stimulation and challenges

I wish I could give credit to the author, but it is anonymous. Just take another look at that list. It is incredible! This is a great list for all relationships. It's a good way to keep friends. It certainly would strengthen marriages. We talked about love (for giving love), hugs, kisses (nonverbal love), using time wisely to be creative and interact with others, to be flexible (take advantage of new circumstances), be willing to be challenged and accept those challenges as an opportunity to grow and learn and enjoy.

What is so beautiful about this list is that it is good for all ages. It is free, no cost whatsoever! Except, of course, giving of your time and self. The beautiful part of it is we all have choices to do the right things. Don't be petty. Take a leap of faith and move on and up!

Always Be Kind

After my husband died, I felt empty. I felt like I was invisible; without any identity. We had been together constantly because we worked together. Even when we got home, we both cooked and both did dishes. I was lost, especially on Sunday. We used to have our grandchildren and family on Sunday. Now he was gone and the grandchildren had moved. There I was with this big table all by myself.

My husband always said he was going to write on my stone, "Here lies Margaret Valone who couldn't stand waste." Well, I don't know what motivated me most. Was it the empty table or the empty life of loneliness? Anyway, I decided to start asking people over for Sunday dinner. There were a lot of widows and widowers, people without extended families. I could be mother, grandmother, or just a friend. It worked. Sometimes we were 8 to 10, or 12 to 14, and the largest group was 20. We had such a good time. The dinner would take half the afternoon. Then everyone helped with the dishes, even the men.

Out of this group evolved a beautiful love story and a marriage. They both had been hurt in previous marriages and now they found joy in each other. I never know who was coming for dinner. I left it an open invitation, but asked them to call so I would know how many to prepare for. Usually, they would call, ask if they could bring a friend and what I wanted them to bring. They provided side dishes and desserts. I did the main course. It worked out fine.

What we were doing caught the attention of a couple of newspapers (even Buffalo) and the story was written up. Because of that, I got a call one day just before Easter 2001. This elderly man called and asked if he could come to Easter dinner. I said of course. Later he called and asked for a ride.

Easter Sunday morning I went to pick him up. I had to help him down the stairs. When I got near him, I realized I had a problem. He was incontinent. The odor was so bad I opened the windows in the car. When we approached my house, I asked him to stay in the car while I got a couple men to help him.

Once inside I said to Judy, "We have a problem." I explained. Without batting an eyelash Judy said, "Well, Margaret, the Lord said we must love the unlovely." How beautiful. The problem was solved. At that very moment the man stood in the doorway and said, "Christ is risen." in three different languages. He was a delightful dinner guest. And I don't know what happened, but nobody smelled a thing.

The following year, three weeks before Easter, he passed away. Just think, if we hadn't accepted him he would have spent his last Easter alone and miserable.

I learned from that experience that when we have an opportunity to help someone by being kind, to grab it. You may never have another chance to do it.

I think I'm going to start a new policy. Laughter relieves stress, so I'm going to make you laugh in every column. I like this one. "Families are like fudge - mostly sweet with a few nuts."

Guess which one I am.

The Joy of Living

People often talk about the fear of dying but not enough about the joy of living. Life is a precious gift. We should live it to the hilt. We were created to be joyful. Get involved with as many people as you can. That's why I went to Helen Ostrye's 100th birthday party. I only knew her and her daughter-in-law Dorothy for sure. As it was, there was only one man I knew from the gang at McDonald's. John had gone to grade school with one of the daughters. That was a beginning. From there on, I just kept meeting people. I got to the party at 2:30 and left at 5 p.m. Nobody suffers that long. I really had a great time!

Another habit I have that makes life interesting is I talk to strangers. I've never really had a bad experience, but I thought of an experience I had last year. I had made up my mind that when I saw something complimentary about a woman, I was going to tell her. Why keep it a secret?

I was standing in the checkout line at Quality Market and this striking woman was ahead of me. She had on a blue cape. I could see long eye lashes and a beautiful complexion, and she had a stylish, short haircut. Her hair was naturally curly. She was a sharp lady! So I patted her on the shoulder and said, "I'd like to tell you what I see when I look at you." I then proceeded with all the things I have written above. She smiled all over the place and thanked me.

Then I said, "I've decided I'm not going to withhold my compliments. If I can make someone happy, I'm going to do it, and I hope they can pass it on." She agreed. Well, then on Sunday, I was telling my son Dan about it during our Sunday phone call.

His response was: "That's all well and good for you, but if I tried it, I'd probably get my face slapped." I hadn't thought of that. Come to think of it, I hadn't done it with men. As for Dan, he could get a slap or worse from a male, too! Sometimes you can't win.

Maybe this story is for women because they are stingy with compliments to other females. (My opinion). An oncologist recently said if we have emotional support and spirituality, the body will take care of itself. This means we should concentrate on the positive instead of the negative. Certainly we spend more time living than we do dying. But of course, we spend more time in death (eternity) than we do in life. Take care of the present now, which will soon be your past. If you make wise choices, your future in death will be beautiful!

I found some cute things to laugh at. Read on:

Gramma went to see Little Johnny, her grandson. He gave her a big hug and said, "I'm so happy to see you, Gramma. Now Daddy can show us that trick he promised us."

"What do you mean?"

"Oh, I heard Daddy tell Mommy that he would climb the walls if you came to visit us again!"

Here's another cute one: A young lawyer had just opened up his firm. He saw someone coming and picked up the phone and pretended he was talking to a client. He motioned to the man to wait. Finally he hung up and asked the young man, "What can I do for you?"

"I'm here to install your phone." Ouch!

A 35-year-old wife had changed her hairdo, her cosmetics and bought a new dress, all to look younger. When her husband came home, she asked him how did he think she looked.

He answered, "Your hair looks like a teenager around 18, your skin looks like 21, and your figure - about 28."

Not a bad report. She thanked him.

The Soup of Life

"Wait a minute," he said. "I haven't added them up yet."

That last sentence cost him a new hair brush, a new window and a week of cold shoulder. The lesson here is - quit while you're ahead, fellas.

Here's a question to think about: how far do you think you're going to go if you straddle the fence? And here's one more piece of advice: "If you do, watch out for slivers!"

Think about this one: "Mud thrown is ground lost." And don't forget some of it sticks to you.

A football coach asked a tryout if he could pass a football. His answer was, "If I can swallow it, I can pass it!"

This is great the hardest thing to give is - in! How true!

On a visit to the zoo a father and son stopped at the stork cage. The little boy asked his father, "How come he doesn't recognize me?"

Every man should work eight hours, sleep eight hours but not at the same time.

Margaret Valone

My Own Soap Opera

It happened on a Sunday. I came home from church and my brother (who is 87 years old and dying from lung cancer) told me he had to go to the ER for an enema. I said, "Nobody goes to the hospital for that." Fortunately, my friend Donna, who works with the fire hall and has good training, said she would go buy some Fleets.

While we waited for her, I set the table and got the food ready for our guests. Donna was true to her word and returned with the Fleets. We sat down and Roddy was in the bathroom. After a few minutes we heard a crash and Roddy had fallen on the floor and hit his head. Fortunately, he broke no bones or bled.

Later that day I started to laugh. I told my brother I was just thinking about a scenario that could have happened. Let's say Roddy died from the fall. When he got to heaven, one of the men at the gate asked, "What happened to you?"

"Well, it was like this, I was giving myself an enema and I fell on my head and here I am."

I can just see the eyebrows going up on the man's face. Then I could hear my brother (who always wants to be the hero) saying, "I was in the Merchant Marine, but it took two fleets to bring me to heaven."

We laughed so hard and we thought we'd like to share this experience with others. We both love to make people laugh, even at our expense.

The Soup of Life

I must tell you another story about this brother. When he was young, he was a boxer before the cancer got to him. He used to do 35 to 40 pushups a day. Now I have a three-apartment house. We live in one, a businessman in another and supposedly four students upstairs. It's always worked out fine except for this year. We have four boys and all their friends who never stop moving and make noise all hours of the night. We can't sleep.

The other night I was sleeping on the porch so I didn't hear the noise, but my brother was annoyed. He went upstairs on his wobbly legs and his loose PJs that were half falling down and offered to take one of the boys up to heaven with him. He had no weapons. It was a comedy. Would you believe one of the boys reported him to the police? I would have loved to see the case come to court. One of the boys is a Marine. I could just see all the sympathy they would get.

Roddy's hospice nurse just howled when she heard the story. She said, "Roddy, if you go to court, call me and I'll bring you some crutches."

Now you can understand why I say, "My life is like a soap opera without the sex."

PHILOSOPHY AND THOUGHTS

How Do You Want People to Remember You?

It's annoying how life teaches you so you can teach others as long as you live. Here's an example: Recently I received a letter from my granddaughter telling me my great-grandson, Liam, lost his cat. While he was visiting Grandma Brownson, two dogs killed the cat. This gave me an opportunity to teach Liam how to deal with death and the importance of making every day count.

I told him how I dealt with the death of a son and my husband. The secret is we must not look at the loss, but instead remember all the conversations we had, the vacations we took, family projects, enjoying sports together, laughing a lot and above all, loving each other in many ways.

Loving isn't only hugging and kissing. We can bake or cook something special. Rusty made an apple pie for dessert when he was twelve. We did things for each other. You can't have true love without respect. So the answer is to concentrate on all the positive memories and put the loss on the back burner.

Now the question each of us should ask ourselves is, "How do I want to be remembered?" Once you come up with the answer, then you must live every day fulfilling those memories. Really, it can give direction to your life. If each family member goes through this same process, it could change the entire household. Include grandparents in this exercise, too. Teachers, preachers, civil servants, like policemen and firemen, all people who deal with people should ask the question, "How do I want the people I deal with to remember me?" It can change our focus and even communities.

The Soup of Life

There's so much going on in the world today that makes me feel helpless and hopeless (for this world, not the next one) that I have to turn my thoughts to my world. There are things each of us can contribute to our immediate worlds.

If you have any ideas for projects our communities can do, please don't hesitate to share. You can call me and I'll volunteer - just don't ask me to run a marathon!

Let's make ourselves aware of how we can use accidents that cause death or injury from drunk driving, drugs that can cause hurt to others and ourselves, unwanted pregnancies that can change your life, divorces that break up homes, bad language that can hurt others and our self-images, etc.

Just like getting over an addiction is to admit you have a problem, so is learning to be aware the first step to a better life.

Do you know how happy you would make me to find out your family, your friends, your co-workers or church family, etc. sat down and discussed this column and came up with ideas to make your relationships even better?

This is encouraging because it's free and you don't need a doctorate to implement the plan. The simple things are the best things.

Would you believe I'm grateful to have gone through the Depression? This experience taught us how not to be wasteful. We used leftovers. Sometimes we came up with novel ideas. We learned not spending is saving. We learned how to save on our utilities.

Kids today don't know how to turn things off. They are very good at turning them on and keeping them on. Is not wasting a good habit? Or is it a necessity? In 21 consecutive days, you can form a new habit. Go for it.

Margaret Valone

I Share the Joy

Life is fascinating if you see it and get involved in it. It's not what happens to you but what you do about it. On March 16, I was very busy. I was asked to be in charge of chapel for the Christian Academy. I had never done this before but I love to interact with young people. I like to tell them about the old days. I want them to realize how far their families have come and how hard they have worked to get where they are. I told them when we were growing up there was no such thing as TV and computers. We had very few toys and made up our own games. I vaguely remember my father used to play this game with us. He'd get on the floor, put a broom under his knees and put two children at the end of the broom. Then he'd pretend he was rowing a boat. All of a sudden a big wave came along, he'd twist the broom and we'd fall into the water! It was so much fun and there was so much togetherness.

We did have a radio and a Victrola that played records. We danced a lot. That was wholesome living. It's learning and sharing.

I told them about my heart problems and how I overcame them. It's so fascinating that I put Jesus into my heart. Then the doctors patched the hole in 1976 and it's still holding! I love the sequence of those events.

In the afternoon, a friend of mine came over and did a lot of repair work for me. He never wants to take money so I treated him to dinner. The dinner was so good! There was actually salt on the steak. I cheated! Then when I went to pay for the check, my $10 gift certificate was unacceptable because the time on it had expired. I had no idea. I thought it was good for a year. I asked the waitress

The Soup of Life

for the address of the owner because I wanted him to know this was not good business for them. Instead of promoting business, they could hurt themselves.

A few minutes later, the manager came out. I have to tell you how he handled it because he was as smooth as silk! I- was seated so he knelt so that we would be eye level. He thanked me for telling him about my displeasure. So many times people will tell others and never come back. He appreciated the opportunity to correct the situation. I was grinning from ear to ear because that's the way I felt when I was in business. He got up from his knees, went to the cash register and gave me back a $10 bill. Did you learn anything?

Now there's a perfect example of everybody doing the right thing and it all worked out. Keep it in mind when you have a similar situation.

Have you ever noticed that there are people who are very generous and very helpful who won't allow you to do anything in return for what they have done? You want to show appreciation. One day I said to one woman, "Why do you deny her the joy you felt when you helped her?"

She looked at me with surprise on her face. She had never thought about it that way. I asked my friend how he supposed these things happened. He said he thought part of the pleasure they receive by doing for others was pride. The people he helped will tell others and their reputation for being a good person will grow.

Maybe he's right, but I think this is a lesson we can all learn. Allow people to show their best side and you can both share the joy. See what I mean?

Margaret Valone

IQ Versus EQ:
Utilize Your Strongest Assets for a Positive Outlook

I told some of my friends that I was going to write a column on IQ and EQ. Every one of them asked, "What's EQ?" Some were college graduates. I'm not surprised. It's so normal to put the emphasis on the wrong things. We all know that IQ stands for intelligence quotient. EQ stands for our emotional quotient. Let's say our IQ allows us to absorb knowledge and wisdom, but EQ enables us to use our knowledge and wisdom with courage and love. After all, what good is all this intelligence if you don't have the ability to share it with others? Let's put it this way - your intelligence makes you a doctor, bit it's your bedside manner, the way you relate to people that makes the difference.

Now, you who have high IQs: don't get so puffed up about it. You were born with it. You can get a few more points through working at it, but basically you are born with it.

Now this is good news for anyone who feels they got gypped in the IQ department. You can develop your EQ as much as you want and it will take you further than the IQ. Anyone can develop the skill of relating successfully with people! Probably the first thing you have to do is forget about yourself. Put the other person first.

I'll share with you what I learned at a Merle Norman cosmetic seminar. It's called the sandwich method. This is how they taught us to sell. I realized this was a formula for making successful relationships!

1. Give a sincere compliment to your prospective customer.

The Soup of Life

Everyone has an outstanding feature. What you are doing in this stage is putting the spotlight on someone else, not yourself.
2. Give them your knowledge of the product (or whatever message you are trying to send).
3. Tell them the benefits they will receive.

One year when I was teaching a Bible class for Intervarsity at the college, I explained the sandwich method this way.

I said, "Let's pretend you are going to meet your girl's family for the first time and you want to make a good impression. You could start out like this: 'Gee, this house has great vibes' (No.1), 'Anyone would be blessed to belong to this family' (No.2), 'If you ever need anything done around the house or any yard work, I'm pretty handy and I'd be glad to help you. (No.3) Boy, you made a sandwich!" Probably every mother who has a marriageable daughter is saying, "Send me one of those!"

I think this story will give hope to everyone. Of course this success story comes with a price! You have to give of yourself. It's a good way to learn to like yourself. Here are some ways you can increase your EQ:

1. Let go and go forth.
2. Don't be afraid of getting hurt. When you do things for the right reasons, reward yourself even though no one else appreciates what you did.
3. Learn to laugh at yourself. When you fell down when you were learning to walk, did you quit? Of course not. Pick yourself up, try again and run! You might even try a good jump!
4. Measure yourself, not by what you have received, but rather what you have done for others.

We all have so much power within ourselves. Let's tap into it and use it.

Margaret Valone

Like a Fine Wine, Life Gets Better With Age

Recently a group of us were discussing the question: Is your life better, easier, or harder as you grow older? It is a good question. Most in the group were saying harder and I was saying easier. They asked me why I thought my life today is easier. I was thinking I have greater peace today than I have ever had. I don't want anything. I don't envy anyone.

1. I don't need a man in my life.
2. Because I'm alone, I don't have to worry about any schedule.
3. I can get up whenever I want to.
4. I can stay up as late as I want. That's usually between 11 and 11:30 p.m.
5. I eat whenever I want to.
6. I can cook whatever I want to.
7. I have fewer clothes to wash, dishes to wash, less work.
8. And now that I'm retired, I don't have to get up and go to work, so I don't mind the winters in Fredonia.

I have a lot of freedom. There's a saying that goes "For every bit of freedom, there is a bit of loneliness." There's an element of truth in that, but I do have a lot of choices on the TV. Although I get so frustrated and disgusted over some of the choices I'm given. There, too, I have the freedom to turn it off. I can make time to listen to music, read or write.

On top of all that, I have friends I can do things with. People have to play a big part in our lives. The more variety there is in the people in our lives, the more interesting our lives are. I like to talk

The Soup of Life

to intellectuals who talk so that we can understand them. If they are using big, uncommon words to appear smarter - that turns me off. After all, the purpose of language is to communicate. We should make everyone feel comfortable in their own skin.

Another thing that makes my life easier is that I'm wiser. I don't let the little things bug me. I do the best I can. I accept my limitations but I want to stretch my life to the limit. Life is still beautiful and exciting. But sometimes when I have the time and the money to do something, I'm no longer capable. It reminds me of a quotation I once read that says "The Lord sends peanuts to those with no teeth." Oh, but we can get dentures!

Now let's look at the things that make life harder as we get older. When we are children we have very few responsibilities. Of course, we have chores at home and we have to take our education seriously. All of a sudden we're adults and we have to go to work. We have to be able to live independently or help out if you get married. This is much easier for females because they can be helpers, but the males are responsible to take care of their family's needs.

Just recently I gave some advice to a young girl who has her eyes on material things. This puts a burden on her husband. I think that most men rate their worth (themselves) by what they do. This is wrong. They I should rate themselves on who they are and their wives should be complimenting them on both. No matter how little we have materially, we should praise our spouses for all they do. (Women like praise, too). We should never let anyone feel they are a failure because of the lack of material things.

What are some of the other things? I can't ride my bike anymore. I can't dance without getting out of breath. I take rest periods when cleaning the house. I can't climb up on the counter to reach things. I can't paint the house like I used to. My husband and I put on the roof together. No more of that but that's OK. I don't own a house now. I miss not being able to swim. I can still shoot baskets, but I can't run. I could go on and on.

Let's look back at the things that have become harder. Do you notice that they are all physical things? The body deteriorates. For the most part, things that pertain to the mind increase (except for Alzheimer's) and the body's flexibility decreases. This is a good arrangement. The body has to deteriorate to die and the mind can help us to live well until we die. Good arrangement. How would you have answered that question? It will be a good topic for discussion anywhere.

Cooking up the Soup of Life

Today we're going to talk about the "Soup of Life." I'm going to give you some ingredients that can make your soup of life delicious!

Some good spices that you can add to your soup of life are: love, praise, kindness, joy, confidence, generosity, trust, humor and faith. You'd better have a big kettle for all of that; and just think you didn't have to go to the store to buy any of them and they didn't cost you a cent. But boy, will they pay off big dividends.

Now let's concentrate on some of the herbs you have to keep out at all costs. These are bitter herbs that don't add good things to our lives. These are the herbs of bitterness: hatred, pain, stupidity, fear, criticism, ugly thoughts and deeds, gossip, uncleanliness in both thoughts and personal habits, sloppiness, irresponsibility, etc.

The first group are positive ingredients and the second group are negative ingredients. The first group will bring you blessings - all for free. The second group are very costly. They will cost the loss of all the positive ingredients.

With the first group, you will enjoy your soup and share it with others. Soup made from the second group will have to be thrown out immediately. Now who in his right mind would choose bitter instead of better? Hatred instead of love? But here's the good news, we have choice. Examine and evaluate all these ingredients. Choose to embrace all the positives and eliminate all the negatives.

I said to a friend of mine recently that I'm in a dilemma. One of the ingredients that makes us live longer is a positive attitude. I don't want to give up my positive attitude, but I don't want to live to be 90 or 100!

He told me I influence a lot of people and they need me. They like my humor. Here's one for you: Don't jump to conclusions, you might break a leg or a marriage.

Let's get back to my soup of life. I have more thoughts about that. Let's try some new recipes. On the second day, I'm going to add more praise and courage to my soup and make sure there are no bitter herbs like envy and jealousy. If you have those on your spice rack, throw them out.

On the third day, I added even more courage and humor. It's time for a big dose of faith (not only in my soup but in myself). So I must be sure to keep fear and doubts out of my soup. And must make sure to leave gossip out of my soup.

On the fourth day, I'm noticing I can add more love, kindness, gentleness, patience, generosity, confidence and good attitudes; but I'm noticing that I have to be very careful not to let things like greed, pride, sarcasm, criticism, deceitfulness, laziness, dissatisfaction (always wanting more), thoughtlessness or causing pain to my soup.

Well, now that I've given you the idea, each of you can become gourmet soup makers. Be sure to check the flavor of the soup and I challenge you to jump into one person's soup today (at least. one) and make that soup tastier. Just think of the impact we can have on our communities.

Speaking of impact, I have a dream. No, I'm not Martin Luther King Jr. and please don't shoot me, but this is the dream. I'd like to see a pilot program for teaching Dunkirk and Fredonia, or even the whole county, a better sense of community. We need a sense of connection and we can help each other out. This dream can become a reality!

Sturdy Foundations Mean Good Marriages

Today we're going to talk about marriage. It's hard to believe that more than 50 percent of marriages end up in divorce! How can that be? What's wrong? What are we doing? What are we not doing?

I'm going to use a principle I learned in Sunday school when I was a young child. This is what we learned as an answer to the question, "Why did God make you?" The answer was, "God made me to know Him, to love Him, to serve Him and be happy with Him forever in heaven." In this case, our heaven will be a happy marriage.

Now let's examine the first part of the answer and notice the order of things. First we have to know the person we want to marry. I'm going to view this from a female point of view, so I won't have to say "he" and "she" every time. But men, this goes for you, too.

How well do I know him? What am I looking for? His attitude? Is he respectful of people? Does he make condescending remarks about females? How does he treat his family? Is he loving and thoughtful of them? Or he can't wait to get out of that house? Is he a worker? How much energy does he have and how does he use it? Is there a balance between work and play? Does he laugh a lot? Enjoy life?

Now how about his habits? Are they endearing or aggravating? Is he clean about his body and appearance? You may think you'll change him after you're married, but that will take a lot of nagging. That may work or may not. Either way, he won't like it. Does he snort? You'd be surprised how a bad habit like that will be annoying. Maybe he has a lot of phlegm that he doesn't know what to do with and he has a medical condition. Would you feel free to discuss it with him? You should. If you smoke and he doesn't, will he try to make you stop? How do you feel about that? And when he realizes how much this bad habit is costing him, he could blow his top, especially if he's tight with money to begin with. Do you both have the same sense of values?

You will have differences. Are you willing to give some latitude on your differences? For example, my husband loved to cook and when he cooked, he cleaned as he went along. I made a mess and cleaned up afterward. After all, if I needed more salt or pepper or shortening, why should I waste time putting it back and forth? So, we each did things our own way. These are little things you can adjust. The one that always got me was the couple who got a divorce because he rolled the toilet tissue from the top and she rolled it from the bottom!

But let's get some things straight. I will not put up with adultery or drunkenness. I expect him to love my family and I will love his. I expect him to be a good example to his children. We will be law-abiding people. There's no room far discussion on these principles.

Well, they got to know each other and she knew she really loved him. Now what follows knowing and loving? When you love someone, you want to take care of all his needs and pleasures. That means you have to work and play together. That's not hard to do. You automatically want to keep his clothes clean so he'll always look sharp, you want him to come home to a house that smells good from all that good cooking that is being prepared and you want the house to be clean and colorful with accents of color. Love and service go together. Service is not a chore, it's a pleasure and it's a two-way street.

What we've done here is look far a good foundation for a good marriage - which is heaven. And if you don't have a good foundation, you know what the opposite of heaven is!

Spreading Cheer

This is a true experience that really touched me. The day was Wednesday, Nov. 30. My gout had finally allowed me to limp around and I had to go shopping. When you're out of bread and milk, you get desperate. I went to the local market. I got out of the car and a woman came up to me all smiles. She handed over her cart. I extended my quarter and she refused it.

"Oh, no!" she said. "This was given to me and I'm passing it forward."

Then she added, all excited, "Put that in your column!"

She was a perfect example of the pleasure of giving.

Then I did my shopping. I was putting my things on the conveyor belt when I noticed the man behind me only had three items. I told him to go ahead and he gave me a big smile. After I was checked out, I noticed I had forgotten my milk. I asked if someone could get a 2 percent gallon of milk for me. A man in line heard me and said, "This is 2 percent, take mine and I'll get another one."

It was wonderful. Everybody was being so kind. Another man found a box for me to put my cans in. Then I got to my car and unlocked it. A woman was just getting out of her car. I asked her if she'd like my cart. She was all smiles as she tried to hand me the quarter. I told her my cart story and I was instructed to pass it forward. I told her I always did this all the time because if I could put a smile on someone's face for 25 cents, what an investment. She said she was going to do the same thing from now on.

I settled in my car with a big grin on my face. Life can be so simple and so rewarding. Everything was so natural and so great. Try it:

We are now into December. Everybody's thinking about Christmas, but how many are thinking of why we celebrate this day? Very few, I'm afraid. A new birth is a new beginning for the person born, but in this case it's a new beginning for all who will accept Him. I think I'm going to try to put in something every week about Christmas. Just a sentence or two to make you think.

Now I'm going to talk to you about gout. I bet most of you aren't familiar with it. I know I wasn't. First I got it in my finger - the middle finger. You might call it the naughty finger, but I never used it like that. I think it's vulgar and besides this finger looked so ugly, I wouldn't give it to anyone! Well, it finally got better. I was putting on some expensive medicine, so it would never come back.

Two weeks later I had it in my big toe! It was all red. My whole foot was swollen! The next day I couldn't put my shoes on. It was a real effort to walk and I cried sometimes. I called up the doctor's office. I thought it wasn't going to come back.

"It won't come back in the same spot," I was told. "Thanks a lot!" I said. "I have a big body here, what can I expect?"

The medicine the doctor gave me started kicking in after two days. I'm now among the living.

Today I'm going to be a guest on the Senior Report with Reed Powers. On the TV show I'm going to try to get churches, families, schools and organizations to provide activities to keep these youngsters out of trouble and give them a lot of praise. Happy teenagers are less likely to do drugs. In line with this thinking it was brought to my attention that there is a group of 75 teenagers who have been recruited by Pastor Sixto. He has brought together this large group and it is non-denominational. One of his favorite activities is playing basketball on Friday nights at the middle school. Now the school has other plans and a basketball court is needed. Any schools that have some free time or anyone else with a court, please help this group out. It has taken a lot of work and people to

The Soup of Life

make s this group a growing reality.

This is why I love doing columns. If we can be used to make things better, then we are successful.

Margaret Valone

WORDS AND LANGUAGE

Let's Talk About Words and Thoughts

Let's talk about words, sometimes the words originate in the mind and sometimes words come to your mind. Either way, they influence the way each of us lives. If we have a positive outlook on life we find it much easier to forgive people who hurt us. We are willing to be merciful. We don't let our pride get in the way. If you haven't learned that humility brings peace and joy and that it is a positive word instead of a negative word, then you haven't matured. You don't have to be old to mature, just wise.

If you haven't learned that praise and appreciation are the backbone of all relationships, you are living a selfish, shallow life. I think of the struggles that go on between spouses that can be eliminated if both of the parties love enough to give up control. When being willing to give up control is exercised, you both win - the person that loved enough to give in and give up and the recipient of this love. The fact that you were willing to concede shows your love for your partner is stronger than your will to dominate. Love never fails. And men, don't think it's weakness to care more for someone else than you care for yourself. You shouldn't divide all the work into two categories male or female. There are a lot of things you can do together. Sometimes you can carry it too far.

For example, I had a tank in the basement in one of my houses and it had to be removed. Guess what? The plumber asked me to hold up the bottom while he carried the top. And there I was with a hole in my heart! Don't say it. I know I had one in my head to match. Another time a friend and I were helping an older man move. There was a dresser with five drawers that needed to be

The Soup of Life

taken out. Of course, it was upstairs and guess who was on the bottom again? They treated me like I was one of the guys. I guess it didn't kill me cause I'm still here. The point I was making was that women can do some male jobs and men can help with the cooking, cleaning, and washing clothes. You can be gentle and patient and still keep your manliness. Next time either of you say "no, that's your job", examine the job, and it will be easier to do it together. So many times when you win, you are really losing part of a relationship. Is it worth it?

I think of two words that go together - arrogance and greed. Of course arrogance and pride go together. Because you are proud you act like you're better than others and the attitude manifests itself as arrogance. A person who is arrogant has few friends and his family keeps their distance as well. That person is unapproachable. If you think you are better than most people you will find it lonely at the top. Let's just imagine what a person who is hateful, bitter, jealous, unloving, and mean looks like? I picture instead of a smile, there's a sneer, instead of laughing eyes there are cold eyes not interested in anyone else. The body is tense, rigid, unwelcoming. This person is not inclined to initiate an opening for a conversation or might not respond to someone else's attempt at conversation. He might even walk away. On top of all of this, his negative attitude is reflected in his face. He has rigid lines around his lips and his eyes are dead. He looks unapproachable. What kind of a life would such a person have? I can't think of anything worse. He would have few friends. He would be a loner. All of this is from his own choices.

I think behind all this arrogance, what starts the ball rolling in the first place, is fear of being rejected. To him this means failure. It's not really. Not if you learn from it. Just pick out someone you would like to be like and study his mannerisms, his conversations, the things (words or activities) he indulges in, etc. Learn to relax. Starting a friendship with a young person might be a good starting point. Do something different. Just remember the definition of stupidity is doing the same thing over and over again and expecting different results. It will be amazing how you think that other people have changed when in reality you have changed.

Let's rub off on each other for positive results. You can change your life - starting today.

Margaret Valone

Maximize Experience through the Mind

The other day I was thinking of ways we can maximize using our minds to enrich our lives and thoughts, and influence how we feel: how we act what we do, what we say, etc. Also, it cannot remain empty or, as sure as God made little green apples, something negative will worm its way into our minds. I see so much beauty in the world! One night the sky was unbelievable! It was shades of blue, ranging from midnight blue to lighter blue, and designs outlined in orange. An artist can copy it, but not create it.

Then there are simple things, like a clean house, that can thrill me. I do it for myself because I can't stand clutter. I can never think in a messy house. I'm not a fuss-pot who makes people feel uncomfortable. I don't make everyone take their shoes off before entering my apartment.

I love artwork. In 1963 when Russ and I went to Paris, where I studied hair coloring with L'Oreal, I walked to the Louvre every day. I can't draw worth a darn! Probably the only thing I can draw is flies, but I really appreciate art. I'm grateful I have a mind that absorbs many different forms of art. I think this can be cultivated!

Take a walk and try to see things you never noticed before. Take a really good look at the people you run into every day. Eyes and teeth make big impressions. Notice the food you eat, or if you're doing the cooking, try to use variations of color. I understand the more colorful food it is, the more nourishing it is.

Try to train the mind to see potentially useful things that are

The Soup of Life

going to waste, and use them. For example, I've been picking up the apples from The White Inn apple tree that no one uses. I bring them to my exercise class and the ladies rave about the apple pies, apple sauce and apple juice. Am I embarrassed when people see me picking up apples? No, not at all. My hatred of waste is stronger than my pride. I kill three birds with one stone:

1. I keep the apples from going to waste
2. I help clean up the yard and
3. The ladies are happy

I just thought of one more - we have fewer fruit flies.

All these benefits would be lost if I didn't think about it or didn't follow through with action. It's all so simple and no one is denying us these opportunities except ourselves.

Let's continue with the mind. Whatever you think about is reflected in your face. You can have a frown or a smile. Your mouth can be soft and gentle or it can be held in a taut, straight line. This is a real negative look or really looks mean. I keep away from people like that. On the other hand, a smiling face is an encouragement to conversation, which, in turn, can be the beginning of a new relationship. The potential is endless and exciting.

I have a great life and I've learned I'm not afraid of death. That makes me a very free person. I have freedom to choose, to act and have faith that my actions will bear fruit. So we're back to the apples again, ha!

You don't have to be a rocket scientist to come up with good thoughts you want to put into your mind and then turn those thoughts into actions. Can I motivate you to try this? I hope so!

Margaret Valone

Open the Lines of Communication Gracefully

Recently a friend of mine said to me that I have used good judgment for my topics. She warned me not to get too serious or controversial. She may be right, but I talk about life as I see it. Unfortunately, all life is not a barrel of laughs. I want to stimulate your brain into new ways of seeing things. Whether or not you act on them is up to you. If we get so that we think alike just think how intelligent we both will be!

I am very interested in communication. Without communication, problems cannot be solved, relationships can't grow and .there can be no understanding and agreement among people. Let's talk about it.

Have you ever noticed that Jews answer a question with a question? Jesus did the same thing. I started analyzing this technique. If someone asks me a question and I answer it, I am in control and imposing my ideas. However, if I turn around and ask them a question, I have given them an invitation to express their views. This is a compliment. I become a listener. Everyone wants to be heard. Once a conversation gets going with a give-and-take system, respect for each other results (usually). I have found that two people may not change their opinions, but they may change their attitudes and progress is made.

Let's try it on our kids. For example, you could be talking about curfews. Your son thinks you are treating him like a child. You want him home by 11:00 on school nights and 12:00 on weekends. You could ask the question, "Why do you think I want you home at those times?" or you could say, "Because I'm the boss of this house and while you live under this roof you either do things my way or move out!"

Don't ever give ultimatums! Let's go back to the first question. He might answer "because you want to show who's boss." Then you explain to him that you are trying to protect him from danger and unwise decisions. You can explain to him that because of your age you have had more experiences. You can't expect him to think like you do since he has not had these experiences. Tell him you love him and ask him to trust you. The longer he stays out the more opportunities he will have to drink and drive drunk or be in a car with a drunk driver. Ask your son, "Do you have the character to say 'no, thank you' or would you offer to be the designated driver? Would you feel like a wimp to do these things?"

If your son or daughter can convince you that they are aware of these things and they can handle temptation and pitfalls, then you have to give them a chance and trust them.

Be sure you let them know if they fail, they have blown it for themselves. It's not your fault. It's theirs. Make sure that they know you choose to have an angry child rather than a dead one!

This technique can be used for all kinds of situations because it opens up conversations. Remember without conversation there is no communication. Without communication there is no cooperation.

If you have methods that have worked for you, please share them with me and I'll share them with the readership. Also you can tell me about things that have failed. Maybe we can change one little thing that will make it work.

Margaret Valone

Positive News Is Good for the Soul

Do you ever get fed up with the media? I mean the press as well as film. It seems that unless something is tragic or threatening it's not worth writing about or filming. Well, Monday's OBSERVER was really refreshing. On the front page was coverage for the local March for Babies that supports national care for babies.

The walk brings together schools, organizations, companies, and just plain people. These people walked to honor and celebrate all the healthy babies that benefit from these marches. Among them were a lot of premature babies. Some babies didn't make it, and they were remembered too. The point is that a few people recognized the need there was for helping newborns who had afflictions. These people are a wonderful example to all of us to get involved in all the areas in which we have interests. Caring, volunteering, and participating can not only save lives, but the good will they create is immeasurable! It gives us a good image in the world too.

Then on the same page was a great story on the program at Ripley School to promote poetry. This is fantastic! Writing of any kind is sharing and communicating. It's a form of self-learning. As you think about your thoughts, you have to organize your thoughts. This also crystallizes your thoughts. Even if you never publish, you will form strong habits for thinking clearly. I am so impressed with the Ripley Schools for doing this! You make it an "in" thing to do. Do you ever think about the music you hear, the clothes you wear and the hair style you wear? Do you really choose them or were you brainwashed by someone who thought they

The Soup of Life

could make money on a new trend? They are thinking about what "they" are going to get out of it. If "they" can have so much power and influence, why can't "we" the people create some positive energy that will benefit everybody? Do you think love is more powerful than hate, anger or fear? I do. So why can't we harness it?

Then the next article was Learning through Service. It was all on the accomplishments of volunteer students, faculty and community partners who have learned through service. They together raise awareness about future volunteer opportunities. Some of the things they have worked on were biological research for improving quality of local lakes, music therapy with the retired community musicians and even some who had never played a musical instrument. I never fail to be impressed at their concert!

When I read the campus does regional cemetery mapping, I thought, "How come I didn't know that? I only hear about the cemeteries being vandalized." This year's celebration is number three, so it's a fairly new program. The thing that counts is it took a beginning to make number three! We should be brainwashed to think new beginnings are so exciting and so rewarding. You don't have to have monumental projects - just little gratifying projects will do. For example, how many lonely people do you know? How could they be accounted for? When I say lonely, I'm thinking of people who wish they had someone or something to look forward to. Wouldn't it be nice if there was a club or agency where you could recommend someone pay a visit and check to see if some socializing would be appreciated? A group could be formed. A variety of activities could be presented. These groups could be in neighborhoods or churches - of course all this would be volunteer. That's a true charity. We can't afford another giveaway program that is paid by the government.

The fun games would depend on the age groups and their health status. I stopped riding a bike two years-ago, but I still shoot baskets until I make one. We have to learn to laugh at ourselves.

What have we been talking about? Life is involvement and relationships. It takes at least two people to make a relationship. Without relationships we are a loner. Loners are lonely people.

Of course, if you like being alone, that's fine. That's called solitude.

If you'd like to make a change in your life, tell someone. Who knows what can be in store for you?

Showing Life's Choices through Actions

Have you ever thought how parents can ruin their children? Last night I was talking to a young girl who has held down as many as three jobs at a time. She bought her own car, pays for the insurance and pays for her college fees. How come this young girl is so strong and dependable? Her mother brought her up that way. She didn't give her every little thing her heart desired and made it clear that she would have to work for what she wanted. Maybe some people would call her a mean mother, but I think she's a great mother. And even though her mother has told her when she graduates from college she will have to find her own apartment and support herself, she loves her mother.

Then I know of some other cases. I became very close to a young girl who came from a dysfunctional family. Her father had a drinking problem. Well, we practically adopted her. We all loved her. She called my husband "Dad" and my boys would break their necks for her. One day she said to me, "If I didn't see it with my own eyes, I never would have believed a family could be like this. But now that I've seen it, I want it."

She married and had two beautiful children. She was a fine mother, a godly woman. Many times, I wondered what would have happened to her if she hadn't seen that she had a choice.

Margaret Valone

Recently, a young man was telling me he came from a dysfunctional home. Between the drinking, the verbal abuse and the physical abuse, it was terrible. Since he never saw anything else, he became abusive, too. It wasn't until he met some good people in his life that made him see he had a choice. He chose to change.

I can relate to these two stories because of the hole in my heart I was born with. My heart would thump, stop, race - you name it. But I had nothing to compare it with and I thought I was healthy, until in 1978 the hole was patched and I saw the difference. Now I can sleep on my left side as well as my right side, and my breathing pattern has changed. I didn't have to catch my breath between thoughts.

People need to know their lives can be better. You can be the person who will show them they have choices just by the way you live.

Are you critical or do you give praise?

Do you have the courage to take the initiative to start a friendship?

I had the nicest conversation with a young man in a wheelchair. I told him I want to travel again and don't know if I could manage. I have a friend who says she'll push me around Italy. "Do you know if there's a light convertible wheelchair that we could use?" That question opened a very nice conversation. He was a good looking young man with a great attitude!

Yesterday someone called me "the Mark Twain of Fredonia." Oh, dear! My mustache must be showing! I better get out the Nair!

Reflecting on the Turning Points of Life

A friend of mine, Nancy S., shared some things with me recently. First, she gave me a one liner. "I have such bad luck with silk pantyhose, they take one look at me and they run!" I know that should be two sentences but that would spoil my "one liner". It's a run-on sentence!

Then Nancy shared with me her early childhood. She was so very shy she hardly said a word until she was twelve years old. At that point she realized if she didn't change, she would have nothing to think about or talk about in her old age as she sat in her rocking chair on the porch. That was her turning point. Today she is very much involved in life.

Our conversation started me thinking. What were the turning points in my life? I've had many wonderful people who have given me great experiences and memories, but I thought of the two biggest turning points in my life. I was thirteen when the first one happened. I was in 8th grade. It was time for me to go see Dr. Crosby for my checkup. When she finished her examination, she bluntly said, "You have leakage of the heart and you can't take gym anymore." Wow! All I knew was that my oldest sister, Grace, had died from leakage of the heart and I was very sports minded so not taking gym was like a sentence! I was crushed. I went home, threw myself on the couch and cried and cried.

When my father came home and found me in this condition, he asked, "What's wrong?" I explained. He answered, "This morning you were well and now you are sick? What has changed? Get up. We're going to see the doctor!" With those words you have witnessed Italian logic and a man of action.

We walked over to the doctor's office. After the examination was over, Dr. Ognebene said "She has a heart murmur. It's very common. Treat her like an invalid and she'll be one. Treat her like she's well and she'll be well." Good advice. My father had some good advice too. He told me, "You are ¼ physical and ¾ spiritual. The mind is everything!" Then my sister Louise taught me that ideas make energy. More good advice. I must have had a lot of ideas because I had endless energy

Another turning point in my life was the death of our son, Rusty. He was electrocuted at the age of thirty. We were very close. Through his death, I received a personal relationship with Christ. I wrote, "I gave him birth. He gave me life." I won't go into it any further at this point. However, if anyone wants to know more, it's all in my book "Life Is Sugar and Vinegar" Call me. I have a few copies.

In reviewing what I have written, a revelation came to me. Here I have recalled two devastating situations that turned out to be great blessings!

Now I'll pull a Paul Harvey on you and tell you the rest of the story. I forgot to tell you in the first story that 39 years later in Cleveland Clinic they found out I was born with a hole in my heart. Now it was the size of a silver dollar. I was patched with Teflon and for the first time in my life, my heart had a normal beat.

Simplify Your Life, Get Rid of the Clutter

As you know, I can't stand waste. In keeping with that philosophy, during the winter, I close off my upstairs and sleep on the couch downstairs. Well, Easter Sunday night it was warm and I decided to sleep in my bed upstairs. There I am in this nice big bed and guess what? I fell out of bed! I didn't know how to handle that much room! Part of me slept on the edge being used to a narrow couch and part of my brain remembered I had a lot of room. At any rate at 3:20 a.m., I found myself on the floor. Good thing my bones are thick like the rest of my body.

Then I got to thinking about what happens when we have more than we need? How well do we handle it? First thing most people would think of is their money. How much shall I save? How much shall I spend? Who will I spend it on? Myself or others? Will I handle it wisely or will I fall off the bed?

As for me, the thing I value most is my time. Time is your life. It is a precious gift. You only get one minute at a time and if you waste it, there's no second (minutes or seconds) chance. I want my life to make a difference to me and a difference to others. If I have to choose between scrubbing the floor or writing a column, I'll write. If I have to choose between cleaning the house or cooking for company, I'll cook. If I have to choose between raking the leaves or going shopping, I'll do the leaves.

I look at my closet filled with clothes. What am doing with all these clothes? Even though I bring lots to the Salvation Army, I still have too many clothes.

One day in church, a new girl said to me, "You have the nicest clothes. Where do you get them?"

I answered, "You should have seen how nice they were 15 years ago when my sister had a dress shop."

I think I should have a private fashion show and try on everything I have. Probably half of them don't even fit any more.

Maybe you spend too much time watching television. I know I do. Usually I just think about two soap operas I'm hooked on during the afternoon, but I just realized I have a lot of evening shows I am partial to also. I need to scale down.

Every year, I ride my bike at least once and shoot baskets at least once. Last year I did neither. The time and the weather got away from me. However, this year I'm going to blow up my tires and blow up my basketball and get those two assignments down immediately.

When do we ever admit we're over the hill? Do you notice how people say "I'm getting old", they never seem to arrive. Or "I'm getting fat." How much fat is fat? Or "I'm losing my mind", but evidently they have found some of it because they never say "I have lost my mind."

Don't Be Shy With Compliments

I like to write about positive things. People are always telling me things. Some are sad stories or cruel stories and others lift our spirits. One day this summer was spirit-lifting time. I went to a graduation party of a young girl whom I have watched grow up. She is very talented. I have no doubt that she will go far. She is innovative and has a head for business.

It's exciting watching these kids grow up. Another young lady whom I have watched grow up is Jennifer Stuczynski. I watched those legs grow longer and longer, but I never dreamed they would take her to the Olympics. She is breaking high jump records all over the world! I have no doubt that she will go to the top! Her parents, Sue and Mark, are very proud of her for who she is, as well as her talent. To think of our having a local girl in a world competition! Now I know that everyone who has Polish heredity is especially proud of her, but don't forget – she's one-fourth Italian! I had to get that in. I hope everyone smiled at that.

And then I had a wonderful conversation with my son, Dan. He and his wife, Dot, had to get as many samples of fragrances they could to be used in testing Dot's Chemical Sensitivity to fragrances. The clerk was so understanding, kind and efficient. Dan took down her name and wrote a letter to the manager, praising her for her dedication to her job and her customers

Then he went to the supermarket and made some purchases. On the way out, he was looking over his tape and saw that he was overcharged. He showed it to the checkout girl and she referred him to the manager. It seems the cereal that was on sale was a different box size. He exchanged them and then when he went to the cashier to rectify the matter, the tape in the machine was causing a problem. The cashier calmly fixed it and took care of all the customers.

Dan was so impressed at how well the situation was handled that he wrote a letter of appreciation to the store. He handed it to the cashier. She figured it was a letter of complaint. When she saw it was just the opposite, she excitedly called the manager over. After reading it, he said, "We don't get many letters like this. I thank you."

Now how much effort did that take? And everyone was happy. I give a lot of compliments to people with big eyes and long eyelashes and small noses. They are the things I don't have. If I don't tell them what I see, will my eyes get bigger, my lashes longer and my nose shorter? Or conversely, if I do tell them, will my eyes get smaller, my lashes shorter and my nose longer? No, of course not, so why are we so silent about giving compliments? I can see some problems. If a man tells another man he has beautiful eyes and lashes, he could get a black eye. If he tells him he has a cute nose, he could get a punch in the nose and because he talked too much he could get a punch in the mouth. Be selective. I think if you tell the mother compliments regarding her children, you'll be OK.

Yesterday, someone called me a philosopher. I appreciated the compliment, but I hastened to remind him I have no degrees or credentials. I just write to the people at large (and they are getting larger and larger!). I don't ever want anybody to think I'm trying to pass myself off as somebody I am not. I'm a nobody - just somebody with a lot of ideas and experience.

The Soup of Life

Choosing Your Words Carefully

Last week on TV I heard about a man who was so mad at the French that he changed his menu from French fries to "freedom fries". Well this morning I had a craving for French toast. I hadn't had any for ages. It tasted so good! Then I remembered about the French fries. Should I have changed my breakfast to "freedom toast?" I don't want to be unpatriotic. Does the fact that I used Italian bread count for patriotic points? It's so hard to be politically correct.

I use this incident to introduce what I really want to talk about. This is the power of words. I think words are delicious! It's fun to think about them and then digest them. Sometimes we have to eat them! Fortunately, they aren't fattening. But they do satisfy and make you grow, but it doesn't show on your body although people notice that you act differently. Let's just think about two word combinations that impact our lives. For example, when you say "I do" it can be the beginning of a beautiful relationship or a prison sentence for life.

"I'm sorry" can heal a broken relationship. "Come home" is an invitation to another chance. Another good combination is "thank you." This always scores points.

Now let's take negative combinations that are harmful. Examples are "get lost", "shut up", and "go home!" These words create problems that may take years to overcome.

Margaret Valone

My friend reminded me of an old saying that says "We spend the first two years of our children's lives teaching-them how to walk and talk. Then for- 16 years we tell them to sit down and shut up! Unfortunately there is more truth than humor in this story.

Now let's look at some three-word combinations like "I love you", "please forgive me", and "you are beautiful". Or, we can say things like "I hate you", "you disgust me", "you are stupid", or "you bore me". The first group is positive and gives us warm, fuzzy feelings. The second group makes us cringe and withdraw. You can almost feel your body shrinking. Can you feel the power of words? Do your words compliment and encourage or do they criticize and hurt people? A good way to check yourself is to monitor yourself for a day. Then when you go to bed ask yourself what kind of day you have had. Are you satisfied or do you think you can do better? Relax and make your choices.

I have a heavy cross to bear. I cannot stand still. To me standing still is going backwards. I have to feel that I am making progress or I am unhappy. This reminds me of a story. How many of you remember the exercises we had to do in grade school to improve our penmanship? We call it "push and pull." The push lines were straight up and down. The pulls were round like a spring or a coil. I did plenty of those. My handwriting was so bad my teachers thought I would be a doctor for sure.

Anyway, the first year we were married we struggled financially. When I felt helpless and hopeless, I did push and pulls for comfort. During this period a young man working his way through college tried to sell me a Collier's magazine. I told him I had no money. He saw my two little boys and asked, "Don't you even have a piggy bank?"

Of course I did. We counted out 300 pennies and he left. Shortly after, Russ carne home and I told him what had happened. He asked if I wanted the magazine. "Not really," I said.

"That's high-pressure salesmanship! Which way did he go? What did he look like?"

The Soup of Life

"He asked me how to get to Cushing Street. Look for a kid leaning to one side by the weight of the pennies." Half an hour later, Russ came home and put three, one-dollar bills on the table. He refused the pennies. I learned how to say "no" to a salesman. Ah, the power of words!

Margaret Valone

The Marvels of Language

Life is a learning experience. After my husband died, I became involved with Intervarsity, which is an international, non-denominational Christian group at SUNY Fredonia. I've kept up that contact for 20 years. They are an inspirational group to me. I had several of them over for dinner recently. We were 12 people and I made mashed potatoes for 24 and it all went! I forgot that kids at that age have hollow legs.

I also took a course for Literacy Volunteers. That was an interesting experience. After I completed the course, I was assigned to a person with a Spanish background. This woman was in her middle 40s. I visited her four times a week and we became good friends. She was doing quite well in her reading, but I couldn't get through to her on telling time.

I had noticed that she was good at making change, so I got this brainstorm of teaching her to tell time with money. I showed her how a penny was one minute on the clock, a nickel was five minutes, a dime was 10 minutes, a nickel and a dime was 15 minutes, and so on. Within two lessons, she understood the concept. You may have an opportunity to use this concept. I love to improvise.

Lately, I've been collecting common expressions, idioms, and colloquialisms. I just had an experience as I looked up the word "colloquialism". A dictionary is great, as long as you know how to spell a word, but how do you find it when you don't know the spelling? If you have an idea how it's spelled, you'll probably find it, but if you're a poor speller to begin with, what do you do?

The Soup of Life

I first became aware of idioms in my French class. Then I turned my attention to Italian idioms and American idioms. For example, one day my brother and sister were having a heated argument. My mother asked what the problem was and Rose told her in Italian, "He wants to be the whole cheese." Just imagine that expression in a foreign language. My mother looked puzzled and dropped the subject.

When someone asks you to do something that is unnatural to your personality, you might say, "when pigs fly!" When a foreigner pictures this, he might think, "those crazy Americans." Then some say to him, "Don't pay any attention to him. He's got bats in the belfry." Huh?

Here are some Italian expressions. When a person has a fine character, it is said he or she is a piece of bread or he's "good like bread." When a person does something stupid, he is called "a piece of stupidity." There is another well-known expression that says, "Call her a tramp first," insinuating before she has a chance to call you a tramp. This means to go on the offensive before you are forced to go on the defensive. Have you ever thought about the idioms we have with the word "bird" in it? For example, "kill two birds with one stone," "he's a bird-brain," "that's for the birds," and "a bird in the hand is worth two in the bush." I wonder why the birds are so popular.

Why do we say "you're chicken" and yet we'll say "he's cocky" just like a rooster, or a cock, struts around. Just the opposite of the chicken. Is that telling us something about differences between male and female?

Let's go back to the dictionary. I was telling my son, Dan, about looking up words and he gave me a lesson. "Look at the word 'dictionary'. The first part of the word says 'diction'. That's what the book is for. It's not a spelling book. Look at the first thing that follows the word. It's all the accents that tell us how to pronounce the word. This book was written by early colonists to make their own language. They wanted it to be different from that of the English. It was intentional."

53

Margaret Valone

Thank you, Dan. I didn't know. Did you? Well, we started with the word "learning" and we learned. How great!

The Soup of Life

Words Have the Power to Change Lives

The older I get, the more I realize the power of words. They can change our lives. Today, I'd like to discuss two words: one is pride and the other is humility.

The dictionary says "pride is a high or inordinate opinion of one's own dignity, importance, merit or superiority whether as cherished in the mind or as displayed in overbearing conduct". There's much more and some of the synonyms are conceit, egotism, self-esteem, vanity (which implies an unduly favorable idea of one's own appearance), advantages, achievements etc. Pride is also often "a lofty, arrogant assumption of superiority in some respect".

There is much, much more. I don't know about you, but I find most of this very distasteful and dangerous. This kind of person turns me off. This kind of attitude for our country is dangerous. If we have to be first all the time, we become feared. I don't want to be feared. I want to be loving and loved.

The Bible says that everyone who is proud is an abomination to the Lord. That's the same word he uses for homosexuality. So what's all of this saying to Christians? Are we to be "proud" of being Christians? Is that what is expected of us? Should we be ashamed of being Christians? Heavens no, but we should value our Christianity by living according to the examples given to us on the way we should live.

We all say, "We should treat others as ourselves." This is good because we are showing humility. We are thinking of the needs we all have and should help others with their needs. Let's look at the definition of humility or humble. It says "not proud or arrogant, modest; to be humble though successful. I am your humble disciple in all things of the spirit. Low in rank, importance, position and quality etc.; courteously respectful, meek".

Now let's compare the two. If you are proud, you can look at humble as a very negative word. It's taking away all your joys. You're doing it to yourself.

Now let's look at humility. You considered yourself a servant. This is good for you because service is so rewarding! It gives you great pleasure to serve others. Money and material things are not your goals. Oh, you don't have to dress like a beggar or not eat food you can afford, but you will be wise stewards of your wealth. Everything is attitude! What a much better world this would be if we changed from arrogance (pride) to humility.

Now there's a third word I want to discuss. The word is wisdom. I value this word so much! Here's the order of things I want:

First is knowledge. This has to come from others. It is not self-contained. Next, I want to turn that knowledge into wisdom. For example, if I learn that touching a hot stove burns my hand, then that's knowledge. If I never do it again, that's wisdom. If I share this knowledge with others, that's love.

Next, I want the vision to see how I can use this knowledge and wisdom and lastly, have the courage to do all of this because my pride cannot keep me from acting on the whole concept. Supposing people think I'm nuts or stupid? Well, let's consider that. Supposing they do? Have you done anything wrong? What was your motivation in acting on this concept? Were you going to make money? No. Were you doing it for yourself? No. Well then, like yourself. If you are doing things for the pure joy of it there will be benefits.

If I deny myself these pleasures, then I am stupid and I can't stand being stupid!

So if I say, "I'm happy to be an American" and I don't say, "I'm

The Soup of Life

proud to be an American," you'll know I'm working on my word vocabulary so that it will be improved. I don't want to be an abomination. I love being a servant. Just remember, a good servant gives a lot of deserved praise to others, but he himself doesn't need the praise to feel worthy. Praise is always appreciated, but we don't need it. I'm a work in progress. I'm getting better. No, that's not my pride. That's wisdom. If you're still learning, like yourself.

Last weekend, in a little more than 24 hours, I went to a graduation party, Chautauqua Institution, and on a motorcycle ride. The first two were common practices, but the last one was very unusual. This young man, Chuck (they are all young when you're 84) comes to McDonald's on his motorcycle and he made good on his promise to take me for a ride. I had no trouble getting on and off and all I had to do was lean in the same direction he leaned; a piece of cake. It was fun!

A friend of mine insisted I write this up because it will be an inspiration to other old people. Look - there's life and there's living. As long as you're breathing, you have life. As long as you are doing, that's living! I believe in living the life!

HINTS

Taking Inventory of Yourself Can Be an Uplifting Experience

The column today is going to be serious.

The purpose is to give you an awareness all of you possess. I hope it will make you feel good and that you will keep it and re-read it every time you need a lift.

Today we are going to take inventory of who we are. Let's start with the mind. The mind is a storehouse of thoughts and ideas. Whether it's a treasure or a cesspool is up to you. Who you let in or what you let in is in your hands. Welcome all positive thoughts and don't allow negative thoughts. Any time you entertain (and it's not entertainment) a negative thought, pretend your mind is a blackboard. Always have an eraser handy and just wipe it all away. The beauty part of this mind is you never wind up with no room. It just expands and expands. It's like a muscle. The more you use it, the stronger it gets.

Next let's look at the eyes. The eyes make it possible to see our loved ones, see the beauty of creation and understand the thoughts of the mind. You can choose to make the ugliness of the world your priority or you can choose to make the world less ugly by using the positive results you have from seeing the beauty in the world. We can not hide our heads in the sand, but we can make sure the beauty that we see in the world is a powerful source to be used for good.

Now let's hear from the ears. With our ears we can hear words of wisdom, beautiful music, the birds singing at six in the morning .or we can hear the restful silence of the day. We can also hear

The Soup of Life

harsh words. Sometimes they come from others' mouths and sometimes they are coming from our mouths. Be careful what you allow other people to put in your-ears and be most careful about what you give others to hear. Here again, we're talking about negatives and positives and choices.

What can we say about the nose? With our noses we can smell fragrances. The Bible says there is the fragrance of knowledge, an interesting thought. You know how I love to cook and have people over for dinner, so of course I think of the fragrances of cooking food. When we look at the fortunes spent on selling fragrances we know that people respond to fragrance. Does your body let out a fragrance or an odor?

There's so much we can say about the mouth. It has taste buds and teeth that we can chew with. It's funny but I always think of words that are delicious and I love to chew on them. We're talking about things that go into the mouth. How about things that come out of the mouth? Are your words thoughtful, loving, kind and positive or are they words of bitterness, hatred, envy, or words of gossip that are hurtful? Here we are again. There is the negative and the positive. We have choices to make.

Now let's consider the heart. The heart tells us how we feel about everything the senses have taught us. Do we have a loving heart, are we kind-hearted or are we faint of heart without courage? Do we have a compassionate heart, or even better a passionate heart, or are we coldhearted? Here again there's the negative and the positive and we have choices. What we choose will move us to action. Be careful. Use the best that is in you and not the worst.

Then there are the parts of the body that give movement. The upper part of the body has an assembly of arms, elbows, wrists, hands and fingers. So much can be done with this assembly! We can work, we can produce, we can hug or caress or we can hit, strike out, and hurt. Isn't it strange that every part of the body can be used for good or for evil? But fortunately we do have choices.

Lastly we come to the assembly of the legs, the knees, the ankles, the foot and the toes. We would be invalids without this assembly. We can walk, run, dance, hold ourselves up straight, or we can kick or go to places that are harmful and hurtful. Choices, choices, choices! Aren't we fortunate that we do have choices? Oh, -I know it's a grave responsibility, but we can rise to the challenge.

Aren't we wonderfully made? Is all this an accident? Maybe our birth was. I know I was. Nobody plans on the eighth kid. But my body was no accident. Do you realize there are no two people alike? No same DNA, no fingerprints or footprints or ears etc., etc. Each of us is unique. It blows my mind when I think of these things.

I think it takes less faith to believe in a creator than to believe a big bang is responsible for all this order and beauty.

If you've been feeling down, take inventory of all your treasures. You have a storehouse, not a poor house. Use what you have and it will grow. Find some positive thinking people who would pick you up and give you new hope.

What Makes You Happy?

Why do I love writing so much? Well, I'm a people person and it's a way of communicating with people without losing my voice. I get such positive feedback from you! I open up new ways of seeing through other people's eyes. Then you have the opportunity to chew on what you read and then decide to swallow it or spit it out. You are in control. Isn't that a great feeling?

Recently, I was challenged to write down 25 things that make me happy. Here are some of the things I wrote:

1. Seeing and holding babies
2. Being with people
3. Listening to good music, everything from quiet jazz to opera and everything in between
4. Beautiful artwork like sun shining through mosaic windows
5. Eating a good meal with people I enjoy
6. Watching sunsets
7. The first snowfall of the year
8. The fairyland created by an ice storm
9. Swimming, the thrill of cutting through the water
10. Dancing
11. I still love to shoot baskets
12. A good movie
13. Reading a good story with a good message
14. The accomplishment of seeing the house neat and restful
15. Laughter - hearing it, making other people laugh and laughing at myself
16. I love being of service, participating in the hospital

visitation program is so rewarding
17. The peace I have through my faith
18. Sleeping in the fresh air every night
19. Having people feel comfortable
20. Networking with people, someone has a problem, you know someone who can help
21. Chocolate can always put a smile on my face and pounds on my body
22. Energy makes me happy. There's so much you can do with energy and not much you can do without it
23. Bringing food to a shut-in
24. Calling up someone who is sick and reading her one of my articles to make her laugh
25. Letting a hot shower relax my muscles
26. Losing weight makes me happy temporarily because I put it right back on

These are 26 and I probably could add many more.

Then we looked at the things I had chosen. Let's see: Mostly, I mentioned people, nature, things that are beautiful to the eyes and the mind, food, and energy. Not one of them was material. What freedom! I don't need a beautiful house, or car, or a big wardrobe, 30 pairs of shoes, etc. As a matter of fact I fear the love of money because I'd become addicted to it, then I won't own it. It will own me!

Make up your own list, as many as you can and then evaluate it. How materialistic are you? Much of your answer will depend on your age. The younger you are, the more materialistic you will be. Having computers, cell phones, CDs, digital cable etc. are now necessities! I see them as burdens. It takes years to shed off the layers of material wants; unless you are smart and disciplined. In that case you can remove the shackles earlier. It's all in the way you look at things. Speaking of looking, stop looking at all those commercials that are trying to suck you in.

I forgot a very important word that makes me very happy. That word is work. I love to work. It gives me a feeling of accomplishment that I'm addicted to. After all, the only difference between work and play is attitude. Just think, you can be a playboy

The Soup of Life

and people will love you for it!

Make your list and check it out. If not having the material things are robbing you of your happiness, maybe you can put them on the back burner and relieve the stress or give them up altogether! You're in control.

Thoughts on Nature

As I'm writing this column, it is Dec. 15. The snow has been falling all day. It really looks like Christmas. To me, Christmas without snow is unreal. The snow gives me a sense of peace.

While I was enjoying the peace, there was a knock at the door and a friend came over to show me a DVD. He knew I'd love it because I'm very much in tune with nature. I love sunsets, trees, flowers, birds, stars - I even named a star "Margaret's star." Why not? Who's going to take it away from me? I'm in the habit of sleeping outside if the temperature is over 50 degrees. I love it, especially if there is a slight breeze in the trees. Well, I kept noticing this one star in the sky between my house and the house next door. It was always there if the stars were out. I don't know much about stars except I can find the Big Dipper. I hated to see this star without a name, so I called it "Margaret's star."

I also love sunsets. If you've never checked out the sunsets at Van Buren Point, put it on your to-do list. Knowing how I love nature, Dave brought over a DVD called God of Wonders. Before you disregard this as a religious tape, look at it for all the beauty and knowledge this tape reveals. It's all in gorgeous color. They show birds, sun, stars, DNA, and snow crystals. Did you know in the DNA there's an enzyme that can repair any flaws in the DNA? Unbelievable.

Here's another bit of information I didn't know. We saw all kinds of lightning patterns that were powerful and I learned this lightning combines nitrogen and hydrogen and they together fertilize the ground so plants can grow. Plants like food and

The Soup of Life

flowers. I never knew this. I never connected lightning with beautiful, colored flowers or our gardens with tomatoes, potatoes, and cabbage - whatever our folks were growing. I've always had respect for lightning, fear, but now it will be different.

There is a segment on birds which is fascinating. They look inside the feathers and one can understand how scientists studied the birds to use principles they learned in building planes. Did you ever stop to think that birds can fly for hours and when they perch on a tree branch, you never see their chests heaving or see them gasping for air? I'm jealous. Thinking of my heart, I learned that squids each have three hearts. Maybe it would be nice to have a backup heart.

You look at all creation and see the complexity of each creature and yet they are all in harmony. They function independently, perfectly and together for one common purpose, to enable the body to function as a whole.

I recommend this DVD to be shown to children, families, biologists and all nature lovers. You can order it by calling 1-877-370-7770. No, I'm not getting a commission.

Margaret Valone

You Can Change Things, Yourself

This week I had my quarterly checkup: I brought my doctor, Dr. Olam, my living will. He was very pleased that I had done this. It takes a lot of stress off those who are left behind, as well as the doctor.

I told him if anything happens to me, don't kill me, but let me go. If I survive, I'd be lucky if my condition was just a little less than before. I'm not going to get younger run faster or enter the Gramma USA Contest (if there was one) or go to jazz band dancing, etc. The past is the past and it's all going downhill, sometimes faster and sometimes slower. If there is anything left that is usable, don't let it go to waste, just so he leaves enough for Michael so I look good. He's an artist and I trust him to hide all the flaws.

You know, I used to think that funerals were barbaric, but when my son and husband passed away, I really was comforted with all the acts of kindness. I changed my mind completely. Besides, now shopping and funeral homes are my social life. Anyway, I encourage all of you to think seriously about making your living will and giving a copy to your executor of the will.

I have some more hymns for you:
* Dentist's hymn: "I shall wear a crown."
* Weatherman's hymn: "Showers of Blessings".
* The Tailor's hymn: "Holy, Holy, Holy".
* Golfer's hymn: "There's a Green Hill Far Away".
* The Politician's hymn: "Standing on the Promises".
* Optometrist's hymn: "Open My Eyes that I Might See".

The Soup of Life

* The IRS Agent's hymn: "I Surrender All".
* The Gossip's hymn: "Pass It On".
* An Electrician's hymn: "This Little Light Of Mine".
* A Single Woman's hymn: "Amen, Amen, Amen".

Now that you get the idea, you can come up with a lot of your own. Now let's change the subject.

Do you ever get depressed after listening to the news or reading it or watching it on TV? People are making such unwise decisions that are changing the lives of millions. Do you wonder how we're being indoctrinated and manipulated? What is truth? The only way I can deal with these situations is to concentrate on the people around me. More than any other subject, I think about relationships and how essential good relationships are. My motto is, "Don't worry about the things you can't change and concentrate on the things you can change." The first thing you can change is yourself. You're probably thinking, "I'm a pretty good person as I am." You're probably right to a point, but is "pretty good" good enough? The answer is no.

While I was shut in with my cough during the winter, I got bored. I decided to call up a friend who was going through chemo and I was concerned about. I told him about the group of us who were going for treatments at Brooks Hospital. While we waited our turn, we got acquainted and started telling funny stories, mostly about ourselves. It sounded like we were having a party. We got to be good friends and looked forward to our get-togethers. As far as I know, they are all still alive. Laughter and good attitude are medicine.

When my brother, Roddy, was staying with me before he passed away, the doctors told him he had about six months to live but he had 11 months. We laughed all the time. He had a great sense of humor, too. My sister, Jo, used to visit practically every day and she has a great sense of humor, so we laughed a lot. I'm convinced that's why he lasted so long. We also had long conversations on Roddy's favorite subject - politics! That kept his blood pressure up. We need to stimulate each other and relationships grow.

Just a reminder to the women. Pay attention to your husband, too. Don't make him feel neglected. Taking care of the children is fine, but dad should come first. Love for everybody will follow.

Men, don't you take being a husband and a father as a beautiful responsibility? Both your wife and your children need to feel loved by you and ladies and children dad needs to know he is appreciated. Show him your love.

How many times have you heard, "She knows I love her" or "He knows I love him, why do I have to say it?"

The answer is that each of them needs to hear it!

The Soup of Life

Fighting the War on Drugs

A while back I was on the senior TV show in Mayville: Mr. Powers, the commentator, said he received a lot of calls from listeners saying they wanted to have me back. He said he will later in the year, but since the show I've received a lot more information and literature, and I've decided to cover a lot more ground from this column which gives me the freedom and space to say what I want to say.

We were talking about the use and abuse of marijuana. Now this is a serious problem which needs a lot of thought. I'm going to throw out some information to you. Think about it, evaluate what's said, then add your two cents.

Here's what concerned Americans, both liberals and conservatives, have said about the war on drugs.

The war on drugs is a failure. Today, the U.S.A. counts for 5 percent of the world's population, but 25 percent of the world's prisoners. We owe that distinction to the War on Drugs, which puts more people behind bars each year.

It's time to face the facts about our nation's war on drugs.
* Conservatives estimate of annual government spending on the U.S. War on Drugs is $51 billion
* Number of people arrested in 2009 in the U.S. on nonviolent drug charges: 1,663,582
* Number of people arrested for a marijuana law violation in 2009: 858,408
* Number of Americans behind bars in 2009 in federal, state and local prisons and jails: 2,424,279 or 1 in every 99.1

adults, the highest incarceration rate in the world
* Number of states that allow the medical use of marijuana: 16
* Estimated annual revenue that California would raise if it taxed and regulated the sale of marijuana: $1.4 billion
* The number of murders in 2010 in Juarez, Mexico, the epicenter of that country's drug war: 3,111, the highest murder rate of any city in the world
* The number or students who have lost federal financial aid eligibility because of drug convictions: 200,000
* The number of people in the U.S. that died from drug overdoses in 2006: 26,000

For more information; go to www.drugpolicy.org.

Here are some quotes on the subject:

"Penalties for the possession of a drug should not be more damaging to an individual than the use of the drug itself." - Jimmy Carter, 39th president of the U.S.

"I'm always for an open debate. . . We ought to study very carefully what other countries are doing that have legalized marijuana." - Arnold Schwarzenegger, Republican governor of California.

"Drug offenders, most of them passive users or minor dealers, are swamping our prisons . . . Yet locking up more of these offenders has done nothing to break up the power of the multi-billion dollar illegal drug trade." - Jim Webb, Democratic senator from Virginia.

"Can any policy, however high-minded, be moral if it leads to widespread corruption, imprisons so many, has so racist an effect, destroys our inner cities, wreaks havoc on misguided and vulnerable individuals and brings death and destruction to, foreign countries?" - Milton Friedman, Nobel Prize Winner, economics.

"We've got to take a look at what we're considering crimes. I'm not exactly for the use of drugs, don't get me wrong. But I just think criminalizing marijuana . . . criminalizing the possession of a

The Soup of Life

few ounces of pot . . . is costing us a fortune and ruining young people who go into prisons youths and come out hardened criminals." - Pat Robertson, founder, Christian Broadcasting Network.

"Never has it been more important to have a national drug control strategy guided by sound principles of public safety and public health." - Barack Obama, president of the U.S.

All of this is valuable information. However, if we don't use it and add our own thoughts, what good is having all this information? I remember a quote that says, "Doing the same thing over and over expecting different results is stupidity!" I couldn't agree more.

Let's go on. Let's talk about the differences between alcohol and marijuana - the effects and the laws controlling each. If you drink too much alcohol, it makes many people violent and they commit crimes. Usually they pay a fine and that's it. We make money and don't spend money for prison costs which are exorbitant! Not so with pot. Pot has a calming effect. These jail arrests can keep you in jail for life! Why such differences? Who's making the money? Lawyers, judges, policemen, people working in the jails, people growing the pot, etc. Are we going to assume that these people are going to risk losing their jails? You wouldn't, so how are we going to level these situations?

Let's ask ourselves, how do we always figure out how to make money by doing the wrong things instead of creating jobs that help our society?

I believe in prevention and cures. Paying money for them is an investment, not an expense!

I'd like to hear more about the 16 states that legalized marijuana. Has their prison population gone down? Have the former users gone into heavier drugs? Are your streets safer? Are you saving money? Making any? We need to know.

We often hear pot users steal to get money for pot. Has that now gone down? They can have a pot plant at home for their use for almost nothing.

I often wonder how many of our congressmen benefit from this problem? Did you know 64 percent of our congressmen are millionaires? They didn't start out that way. Is money (the love of money) now our god? Does either party care about us? How do we get people from grassroots to get back the power? And if we do, will they become like them? Wouldn't it be wise if we could make strides locally and then reach the ears of states and the federal government? If we think we are powerless and don't try, then we are powerless by choice.

Are we going to step up to the plate or are we going to be stupid and keep things they way they are?

Let's Make Our Society Better

This is the first of five columns concerning what's happening to our society and what each of us can do to make things better. I know we can't save the world, but we can make a difference. If we can change ourselves and our little corner of the world, we have made a contribution. Let's consider what I have written. Then talk to your family, friends and community leaders, and then let's set a course of action.

I want you to sit back and really think about this column very seriously. Each of us is a part of society. We play many roles. It's time to take time to consider if we are contributing to the problem or trying to correct our condition. We've got to try harder! We usually say our society is made up of the family, the schools, our churches, and our governments. So let's start with the family.

So mothers, here are some questions that need to be asked: do your children know that you love your husband? They can see by the way you look at each other, talk or yell at each other and your concern for each other. This is crucial.

I used to tell our boys that their father came first. I got a lot of flack for saying that, but I figured if they knew we were tight, that would give them a sense of security. Years later, psychologists said the same things. When our boys were older, I asked them if they felt slighted because of what I had said. They said, "Not at all." By the way, this attitude could be good for the marriage, too.

Now moms, ask yourselves the following:
* How many times do I tell my children I love them?

* How many times do I praise them?
* Do I give them opportunities to earn praise?

You don't have to bribe them to get things done. Just ask. I have heard both mothers and fathers say in disgust and some anger, "Don't they see what needs to be done? Why should I have to ask?" The answer is that you are the adult and see things they don't see. Instead of ordering them, ask for help. Give them a chance to be heroes.

1. How do you reward them? (a) Praise is cheap but the most valuable. (b) Cook a special food. (c) Get a video they want to see. (d) Plan something special like a picnic or a trip. Be creative.
2. Is laughter common in your house? Do people like to come to your house? (Especially your husband.)
3. This question is a biggie! How do you handle discipline problems? Do you ignore them or say, "Wait until your father comes home?" Or do you lay ground rules from the beginning? Sending them to their room is no punishment at all if all their toys (TV, computer, etc.) are there. Do you take away some privilege or some event they really want to see? Hit them where it hurts, figuratively speaking. Be firm. Once they know you will stand firm, things will change. Be sure your husband backs you up.

Most of what I've written applies to single moms, too, but of course you'll have to make some adjustments. Don't try to do it alone. Get help from your family, friends and church.

The reason I've gone to so much trouble to spell these things out is that lately I have heard horrible stories about mean, hurtful mothers who didn't nourish their children and they had problems adjusting in life. How could you want healthy relationships when you've never seen one? If you have or had a good mother as a role model, let her know how much you appreciate or appreciated her.

Mothers, after you have examined your role as a mother, be honest with yourself and see where you can make amends or changes. Ask your kids how they felt and feel. You can make your relationships even better. Don't be afraid or too proud to say, "I'm sorry. I'll try to do better and I'm keeping an eye on you to make

The Soup of Life

sure you don't make the same mistakes I made."

Just think of criticism as an opportunity to improve. Besides, you're the one that asked yourself these questions and nobody else knows your answers!

My goal in writing this particular column is to get families talking about themselves and making necessary changes. I want all the readers to do this and let there be a positive results from new actions.

I'd like to see panels made up of parents, students, teachers, administrators and government leaders to discuss "Living in America Today." Could we have assemblies in school covering these subjects?

I'm going to continue coverage on all these areas. Get ready, men. You're next!

Margaret Valone

HUMOR

Learning through Laughter

So many of you had a chuckle over my cabbage story. This triggered a memory of one of the best operators we ever hired. Her name was Janie. She loved to cook. She practically lived with us, so she cooked a lot for us. Her secret for being a good cook was: "first-you-sauté-the-onions"--no matter what you cooked. We loved her cooking, although sometimes I used to tell her she should open a restaurant for the blind.

Janie had a terrific sense of humor. We used to love to improvise! I was Abbott and she was Costello. One day I said to her, "Let's pretend I'm a salesgirl and you come into the shop to buy a dress." She agreed. Then I started my pitch with the question, "What kind of an affair is it going to be?"

"Oh, I don't have affairs! What kind of a girl do you think I am?" Then it went on from there.

My husband used to come out with unexpected remarks. One night he said, "You belong to so many boards you could build an outhouse." That didn't sound too good so I asked him to change it to a "small garage". Semantics is everything.

What do you think you need to have a good life? I came up with a formula that guarantees a happy life because it all depends on each one of us and no one can stop you.

Here goes: First of all, you need an active mind followed by a loving heart, followed by willing hands and feet.

I put them in that order because I started at the top of the body

The Soup of Life

and worked my way down. Actually, the action could originate in the loving heart. There has to be great connections between the heart and the head.

I've heard people say that there are only 18 inches between the head and the heart. I don't know how accurate that is, but at any rate, it's not much, but oh, so vital. All relationships start with this connection. I think of the mind as a machine that is capable of doing all sorts of things, but machines have to be plugged in or need fuel. That's where the heart comes in. If you have a passion for something, the possibilities are endless. How's your heart condition?

Now we have the machine and energy source and we need hands to run the machine and make the product or the result. Then we need feet to work with the hands and finally deliver the product. Sometimes they are tangible products and sometimes they are ideas that will make others feel good. Think of all the people you can impact today. Call them, compliment them, show them you care. The product could be food or service or transportation. Use your imagination. I feel better already.

Laughs, Peppered with Some Groans

I'm exhausted! Would you believe I sat down to write to relax? I have been looking for our wedding picture. This means I have to go through umpteen boxes to look for it in the basement. I didn't find pictures, but I found histories about hairdressing, the bicentennial, and the sesquicentennial. There are pictures, too. I'll have to organize the material and we can reminisce about those days. The basement was yesterday. Today was upstairs. I found all kinds of pictures on our Italian tours and my visit to Malaysia. That's another story.

I also found some material I had set aside for my third book, but I've given up on that. My computer expertise is very limited. I was working faithfully and carefully every day. I had quite a bit of it done. Then one day, for some unknown reason, I wiped everything out, never to be retrieved. I sat down and cried. Then I gave up on the whole thing. However, today I found some funny one-liners, so today's column is for laughing and groaning. Here goes!

* A bicycle can't stand on its own because it is two tired.
* Did you know the definition of a will is a dead give-away?
* Time flies like an arrow. Fruit flies like a banana.
* A backward poet writes inverse. How about revise?
* She had a boyfriend with a wooden leg but broke it off.
* I like this one - A chicken walking across the street is poultry in action.
* Be careful to pay your exorcist or you can get repossessed.
* With her marriage she got a new name and a dress.
* Show me a piano falling down a mineshaft, and I'll show you a flat minor.
* When a clock is hungry it goes back four seconds.

The Soup of Life

* The man who fell into an upholstery machine is fully recovered.
* A grenade thrown into a French kitchen would result in Linoleum Blownapart.
* You feel stuck with debt if you can't budge it.
* He often broke into a song because he couldn't find the key!

Enough of that. Now I'll give you some worthwhile quotes from Eleanor Roosevelt:

"Many people will walk in and out of your life, but only true friends will leave imprints in your heart."

"To handle yourself, use your head - to handle others, use your heart."

"Anger is only one letter short of danger."

"Great minds discuss ideas, average minds discuss events, small minds discuss people." (For the last example, I'd change "discuss" to "disgust.")

"He who loses money, loses much. He who loses a friend, loses much more, but he who loses faith, loses all."

"Beautiful young people are accidents of nature, but beautiful old people are works of art."

"Learn from the mistakes of others - you can't live long enough to make them all yourself."

I love this next one because when I visit the sick at Brooks Hospital, we love to make a circle. Here's why: "Friends, you and me... you brought another friend... and then there were three... we started our group... our circle of friends... and like that circle... there is no beginning or end."

She quoted this often, too: "Yesterday is history, tomorrow is a mystery, and today is a gift; that's why they call it the present."

Many people loved President Roosevelt and many people hated

him: But I think most people respected Eleanor Roosevelt. Hey, I don't look at who says something, I look at what is said. Then I judge for myself.

Recently, I watched a situation unfold. The people who represented one point of view saw themselves as high-minded. The opponents saw them as high-handed. Both are part of the body but they are worlds (and words) apart. Interesting.

Now let's laugh--can you imagine telling someone you care about these jokes?
* May your life be like toilet paper, long and useful.
* Shoe factory fire - more than 200 soles were lost.
* The butcher backed into a meat grinder and got a little behind in his work.

Laugh Often

I'm reading a book on increasing your immune system by eating broccoli, yogurt, and garlic. Also people who laugh more actually have stronger immune systems. This helps in resistance to colds or infections. It also is key to ending painful inflammation, preventing or slowing heart disease, even fending off deadly cancers.

When my brother Roddy told me he had six months to live from lung cancer, I took him to live with me. We laughed all the time remembering things we did as kids. My sister Jo joined us a lot and she had stories too. He lasted 11 months and they were good months.

Now, I'm going to teach you how to laugh. It's more fun if you do it with friends, but if you live alone, go in the bathroom and pretend you have something funny to laugh about. You start this fake laugh and before you know it you're really laughing and you can't stop for awhile. I bet three times a day would be good. Now if you're a good sport you'll share your secret. Of course if you're too proud, you'll keep it to yourself. If I tell it to someone and they say, "You're nuts," I say, "Thank you. Nuts are good for your health too."

I just tried it out on a friend. I called her and said, "I'm going to make you laugh. It's good for your immune system." Then I started laughing. In a second she was laughing too and we couldn't stop. We're going to do it every day at least twice a day. If you need a partner, call me. I don't think I can overdose. I'll tell you what, from now on every time we meet, don't give me a smile - give me a laugh. Let's see what happens. I'll know if you're reading the column

Now I'm going to make you laugh. A reader sent me these one-

or two-liners.
* The invisible man married an invisible lady. Their kids were nothing to look at.
* Does a true vegetarian eat animal crackers?
* A prisoner has crashed into a cement truck. The police are looking for a hardened criminal.
* A 50 lb. bale of human hair fell off a truck downtown. Police are still combing the area.
* Twenty-five toilet seats were stolen from the police station. The case is still unsolved because the police have nothing to go on.

I know that laughter is good for your health, but do groans count against your health? We should probably make just as hard an effort to get rid of the negative as we do to embrace the positive.

My daughter-in-law, Barbara, sent me a quote from the writer Joy Tinsley and Joy gave Barb the information in person. I enjoyed it and I think you will too.

"I have never been afraid to grow old - in fact I wanted to embrace aging. It's very simple - as you grow you learn more. If we stayed at 22, we would always be as ignorant as we were at 22." (and I was plenty ignorant). "Aging is not just decay, it's growth. It is more than the negative that you're going to die, it's also the positive that you understand that you will die, that you live a better life because of it.

When people keep on harping and whining about aging, to me it reflects an unfulfilled life that hasn't found meaning. Because if you're at peace with yourself, your God and with all mankind, you don't want to turn back - you want to move forward. You want to see more, do more and be more. I've decided I'm going to live or at least try to live with dignity, with courage, with humor, with composure."

The culture we have does not make people feel good about themselves. We're being fed a lot of wrong things and we need to be strong enough to say, 'If the culture isn't decent don't buy it.' You don't have to be young, slim, sexy and rich to be happy.

The Soup of Life

I want to continue surrounding myself with loving, caring souls - my family and friends."

I like her attitude. That's good advice for any age, any era. I especially liked when she wrote, "aging is not just decay - it's growth". That's if you collect all the wisdom you can, use it, spread it around.

Thanks, Barb.

Margaret Valone

Finding Laughter, Happiness and Health

Recently I watched a panel of five very successful people on *The Larry King Show*. They talked about how to be happy, healthy, wealthy, and spiritual. It was very interesting. Everything starts in the mind. You have to know what you want and visualize it. One of the men on the panel got rich from the *Chicken Soup for the Soul* books. The first book was rejected many times before a publisher took it. He says you have to be persistent, even if it takes 100 times. I wonder if I wrote a book called *Pasta for the Soul* or *Pasta for the Stomach*, do you think I could sell it?

Seriously, though, I'd like some input from you. A reader recently said to me, "If you think you're dying, please leave 100 columns behind so we can still read them." She wants me to become a ghost writer!

This got me thinking. If I produced a book with some of the best columns, do you think it would sell? You've already read them. Would you re-read them? Do you think the columns would be interesting to readers at large? Please give me some feedback.

Now let's go back to the panel subjects. First let's tackle happiness. They said you have to laugh at least four times a day. I've told you before that scientists say adults laugh eight to 12 times a day and children laugh more than 100 times. Who's teaching whom?

Another way to find happiness is to let go of the anxieties you have. Let's separate "the wants" from "the needs." Don't forget - laughter is contagious. Surround yourself with happy people. For

The Soup of Life

example, last Friday a friend called up and said, "We're having a goulash party at your house tomorrow. I'll bring the goulash."

"OK. How many people do you want me to invite?"

"I don't care. I have lots. At least 12 people."

Well, we wound up with 14. One person brought fresh Italian bread and butter, another a crock-pot full of meatballs, and soda pop, two brought salads, and another brought brownies for dessert. We had a feast! And we pulled it all together in less than 24 hours, including sleep time. It's so much fun to be spontaneous! Try it!

Now let's talk about being healthy. I'm a walking example of how healthy thoughts produce healthy living. I was born with a hole in my heart, but I always considered myself healthy. I did everything my friends did.

I told my sister I'm going to think "tall and skinny." I want the three inches I've lost back and I want to lose the 20 pounds I've found. So every day I pat my stomach and say, "Go away", and I take a deep breath and stretch and say, "Get tall". So if you see me and you don't recognize me, it's working. If Michael has to get an extra long coffin for me, that would really be a hallmark of success!

They didn't talk about the topic of spirituality. A real growth in spirituality is to make your relationship with Jesus personal. Talk to Him. It's a start.

Here are some things I ponder:

Why is it the shorter the time you have left in your life, the longer it takes to remember things and the longer it takes to do them?

Why do people spend so much time on euthanasia and so little time on our youth?

Why do schools have such a hard time coming up with a dress code? Could it be they couldn't decipher the code?

Margaret Valone

Yesterday I had to clean my dirty phones. How come they get so dirty, when I never talk dirty?

Learning through Humor

I thought I'd share some of my favorite jokes with you.

There were two brothers. One was going to Florida to vacation and he asked his brother to take care of his cat while he was gone. He agreed. One day, the brother in Florida got this call:

"Your cat is dead."

"What? I can't believe this! What a shock! Is that the way to tell something tragic to a person?"

"What should I have said?"

"Well, you could have said something like this, 'Your cat climbed out on the roof. He tried to jump to the tree. He didn't make it. He fell and broke his neck. I took him to the vet, but it was too late!"

"Gee, I'm sorry. I'll never do that again. Thanks for telling me."

The next winter, the brother went to Florida on his usual winter vacation.

One day he got this call from his brother, "Mama climbed out on the roof ... etc."

It's so stupid, it's funny.

I always liked the one about the pessimist and the optimist who owned adjacent farms. Every morning, the optimist would say something like, "What a beautiful, sunny day."

The response would be, "Yeah, it's going to get so hot our crops will probably dry up and die!"

If it rained, the optimist would say, "This rain is just what our crops needed!"

"Yeah, it will probably last for days and we'll be flooded out!"

The optimist decided to teach his neighbor a lesson. He invited him to go duck hunting because he owned a very special dog. So they did. The optimist took a shot and the duck came down. He ordered the dog to fetch the duck The dog did. Instead of swimming over, the dog walked on the water!

"There! Did you see that?"

"Yeah, the dog can't swim, can he?"

I laughed at this, but at the same time, I can cry over all the people who never see the positive side of life.

Last night at prayer meeting, we had a new leader. He said this was not his favorite thing to do. I explained to him that he's not alone. Surveys show that speaking in public is the number-one fear. The second is the fear of dying. He retorted, "Then the ultimate fear would be having to deliver your own eulogy!"

Isn't that witty? I jus have to give credit to Bob Scudder for this one.

Here's one I never forgot. This young girl was telling us about a dress a girl was wearing the night before. It was so thin and she wasn't wearing a slip. She remarked, "Her dress was so conceiving!" There was probably more truth than error!

Here are a few things to think about:
Learning from your experiences is intelligence. Learning from other people's experience is wisdom. For example, if you learned that touching a hot stove burns your finger so you never do it again this is an intelligent learning experience. On the other hand if you believed your mother who told you not to touch the stove and spared yourself the pain of the burn, this is wisdom.

The Soup of Life

If you ask yourself in a certain situation, "Should I or shouldn't I?" You already have your answer. When there is doubt, don't do it! This rule of thumb will serve you well.

Cigarette smoking robs you of your health and your wealth! You can't afford to lose either.

Are you going to be intelligent or wise? Wisdom is much better. The choice is yours. Do yourself a favor and think about all these things.

Margaret Valone

Embrace Your Sense of Humor

Recently I talked to the residents at St. Columban's on the Lake. It was so much fun! First I asked them if there was anyone there under the age of 80. There were none. I said, "Good. Now I don't have to talk about safe sex." We all laughed. Then I told them that adults, on the average, laugh eight to 12 times a day so I wanted someone to count how many times we laugh in the next half hour. The count was 22 times! Great! Since laughter is like medicine, I felt like Dr. Valone. If they hadn't laughed much, then I was just a pill.

Then we concentrated on the topic of the day: "Life is What You Make It". I like to use this topic because it pertains to all of us and once we're aware of this topic, we can choose to make a better life. It all goes back to the fact that for every action, there is a reaction and we do have choices. I will say this again and again until you learn it. Every teacher knows that the best way to teach is repetition.

I hope I haven't told you this story before. It happened years ago when I was planning a tour to Italy. I had to go to the travel agency. I was wearing a mauve short set. It was nifty, sharp, or awesome (take your pick). When I entered the agency, one of the workers said, "What a cute outfit!" This was great. Who doesn't like compliments? Well, when I got home, I looked in the mirror to admire myself and I gasped! There, thrown over my left shoulder, was a dish towel! No wonder she admired my outfit! There wasn't another like it in the world! Then I thought of all the money I could save. All I needed was different towels to change the outfit! I

The Soup of Life

laughed like crazy. What would we do without a sense of humor?

Now let me share this with you. Some of you who are computer smart have probably seen this. But for the rest of us who aren't, here goes.

> "It is with the saddest heart that I must pass on the following news. Please join me in remembering a great icon of the entertainment community. The Pillsbury Doughboy died yesterday of a yeast infection and complications from repeated pokes in the belly. He was 71. Doughboy was buried in a lightly greased coffin. Dozens of celebrities turned out to pay their respects, including Mrs. Butterworth, Hungry Jack, the California Raisins, Betty Crocker, the Hostess Twinkies, and Captain Crunch. The gravesite was piled high with flours. Aunt Jemima delivered the eulogy and lovingly described Doughboy as a man who never knew how much he was kneaded. Doughboy rose quickly in show business, but his later life was filled with turnovers. He was not considered a very smart cookie, a little flaky at times. He still was a crusty old man and considered a roll model for millions. Doughboy is survived by his wife, Play Dough, two children, John Dough and Jane Dough, plus they had one in the oven. He is also survived by his elderly dad, Pop Tart. 'The funeral was held at 3:30 for about 20 minutes."

Gee, I wish I had written that! So clever and so funny!

I'll leave you with a thought for the day. Don't let life get the best of you. Just remember that Moses started out as a basket case.

Margaret Valone

Finding Humor in the Operating Room

I was wondering when I'd find something comical about my heart surgery. It all started a few days before I came to Hamot Hospital. I decided to color my hair for the occasion. I used light-ash brown. When I shampooed it off, my hair was black. Trying to go lighter on a dark base is a hairdresser's worst nightmare. I'd have to wait for it to wear off. Much to my surprise, everyone liked it and said I should keep it that way. I was afraid my doctor would think he had the wrong patient.

Did you know that Hamot Hospital provides a free stay at the Avalon Hotel for their heart patients and their relatives? Really. And they give you valet parking too. In the morning, we had to take the 5 a.m. shuttle bus because preparation work had to be done and the surgery started at 7 a.m. All the while I was under, I was dreaming of horror stories on TV. I also told my family I was cooking eggs in Poland. My "grandson", Nathan Cooper, is getting married in Poland in August. I want to go.

Well, you will never believe what happened to me in the operating room. There was a small bubble that burst in the lung. I was all swollen. My left eye was shut. I looked like I had been in the ring and lost. On top of that, my voice sounded like I was on helium. One morning, a repair man was drilling a hole. My gown was slipping off my shoulder, and it looked like I was winking at him. I yelled, "No, no, I'm not winking!" When my friends came to see me, they all laughed. I looked like I had gained 100 pounds. And when I talked, they really cracked up. One of them said, "This will give you fodder for your column." I said, "I've got news for

The Soup of Life

you. - I have enough material for my 'mudder', too." If I rub any part of my body, it feels like there are Rice Krispies under the skin. It will go away in time. In the meantime, I look like a cartoon character and sound like one of the Chipmunks.

I had some good news, too. My mitral valve was not leaking and neither was the aorta. The doctor just did three by-passes. I can't describe the beautiful care I have had in this hospital. I asked a student nurse named Gabriel why he took up nursing. He answered, "I've always wanted to be a nurse. I guess it's because I care so much!" In my opinion, that's the best possible answer!

In Erie, Pa, it didn't matter if you were a housekeeper, office worker, technician, or doctor - everyone showed concern and interest. Even the patients and their relatives showed an interest in each other. Even though I came out with a fat face and a funny voice, I truly had a wonderful experience.

I cannot end this column without giving thanks to Dr. Tak and his staff at the Dunkirk Health Center. Brooks Memorial Hospital did some of the testing for Hamot Hospital. The insurance companies of New York and Pennsylvania also made a cooperative effort. Now that I'm home, all of my local friends and family are spoiling me. It's great to be alive!

Margaret Valone

A Dose of Humor

Last week was a serious column. One man called me and said he never misses my column, but this one was the best I've ever written. Another told me I was a philosopher. The women said nothing. Maybe they already knew all that stuff. Anyway, today I'm going to make you laugh. Be sure you have your water ready, because laughter is like medicine. Here goes:

* A sign in a doctor's office: God heals. The doctor takes the money.
* Adam and Eve had a good marriage because they had no in-laws.
* What's the difference between in-laws and outlaws? Outlaws are wanted.
* When you have a raft of kids that are driving you crazy, what can you do? Put them in the water and give them a paddle.
* A kindergartner said that Groundhog Day is the day Jesus comes out of his cave and if he doesn't see his shadow, he goes back in.
* You can't beat a good wife. Unfortunately, you can't beat a bad one either.
* Did you hear about the women who prayed for a dishwasher and her daughter moved back home?
* She was so busy giving people a piece of her mind that now there's nothing.
* One week when everything was going wrong a friend tried to cheer me up. My friend said, "Just look at Job." "Yeah," I said, "but I don't want to give him competition!"

The Soup of Life

* She lumps all spiritual things together and then can't swallow it.
* Just remember: a Christian is not brainwashed but blood washed.
* There are too many wise guys and not enough wise men.
* Bitterness is like taking poison and hoping the other guy will die.
* Television programs cover us with filth and then they try to sell us soap! (I like that one!)
* If you can't brighten a person's life, would it be too much trouble to bless a person's day?
* Live your life well so that in the end, the Lord will say well done and not half-baked.
* He never would fly because the Bible said, "Low, I will be with you always."
* When you blow your own horn, all the notes fall flat.
* He is an artist painting for the color blind.
* She's a singer singing for the deaf. Or, I remember Rudy Valle, he sang in the silent movies!
* Whenever you say someone is so stubborn, it's because you're pushing just as hard in the opposite direction!
* Have you ever made a trip and missed the journey?
* If I don't die laughing, I'm not dead. Don't bury me. Get a second opinion.
* The music of life is playing, but you're too tired to dance. (I like that one. Sad but true).

I have a nephew who is a biology professor. One day he said to his wife, "I'm thinking about being cremated and having my ashes put in the sand at Van Buren Point. Then people can say Jeff got in my hair when he was alive. Now that he's dead, he's getting between my toes!" (We all have a sense of humor in our family).

Margaret Valone

Philosophies That Tickle Your Funny Bone

Hello. I have been given a wonderful opportunity to reach the readers of this paper. What can you hope to hear from me? I will confess to two of my secret ambitions and they might give you some clues.

When I was very young I wanted to be a teacher - that was going to be my ministry. Now that I'm older (as in old), I've had a secret ambition to be "The Grandma Moses of Comedy". I love to make people laugh. On the other hand, I'm a philosopher. I love to think about things and to learn new concepts.

Let's start with the comic side. A few years ago I prayed about doing stand-up comedy. I asked for a sign. Well, that year I was invited to three organizations to do comedy routines and I was asked to do seven eulogies. "Please, God", I explained, "I only wanted to knock them dead, not bury them!" Now I have been given another chance.

Before I go any further, I must ask male readers to bear with me. Sometimes I pick on men for my jokes, but when you read my philosophy on the role of the man in the house, you will forgive me. Please hang in.

Let's start with the beginning of Creation. God made Adam out of dirt. Do you suppose that is why there are so many dirty old men? On the other hand, Eve was made from man's rib and women have been ribbing men for years, only it's called nagging. I wonder where the term "the terrible twos" came from? There's no record of Eve's saying it. There's no record that she ever washed

The Soup of Life

fig leaf diapers either! Speaking of children; the thing that impressed me most in Italy was the way the parents obeyed the children.

I study human behavior and I notice things.

Why do you suppose men get married later in life and die younger than women? Could it be marriage agrees with her and kills him? It is said man is incomplete before marriage. Then he's finished.

Let's talk about dieting. Have you ever noticed that when a man says he's not half the man he used to be, that he is twice the size he was? I went on a diet once for 14 days - no bread, no sweets, no eating between meals, etc. At the end of 14 days, I lost two weeks, I lost my temper, I had lost my mind, but there was no reward on my scale.

Sometimes the way you say things makes a difference. For example if a woman has such an ugly face, she could stop a train, you might discreetly say, "She's in traffic control".

Here are some things you could say to a friend who is showing you her new baby and it's ugly. "What a big baby! I can't believe this is your baby! Now THAT'S a baby! I'm sure this baby is one-of-a-kind."

Have you ever wondered why a woman would prefer beauty rather than brains? A very discerning customer I had answered, "Because she knows men can see better than think!"

I hope I've made you smile or even laugh out loud. If you did, tell the editor. If you didn't, well, you haven't seen my serious side yet.

Margaret Valone

The Art of Conversation

An "adopted" grandson of mine has brought home his fiancée from Poland. Fortunately, she speaks English well, but she has opened our eyes to all the expressions we use that, when translated literally, they don't make sense. Let's look at some.

When a foreigner hears us say, "he kicked the bucket," can you imagine what they visualize? Or, "she hit the ceiling" (with her head or her hand?), "he thinks he's a big shot", "she's green with envy", or "he's got bats in his belfry." What's a belfry? When a person rubs you the wrong way, does he have to go to massage school? "They just blew their money." "It blows my mind." "You made a sucker out of me."

Here are some animal sayings; "that's for the birds", "let's talk turkey", "in a pig's eye", "don't horse around", "I'm dog tired", "I'm working like a dog." Dogs work? "She has a memory like an elephant", "he's slippery like a fox", "she's a foxy lady", "I'll believe that when pigs fly", "you can't beat that with a stick", "he just can't cut it", or "his head is in the clouds".

Try talking for five minutes without using a verbal expression. We have no idea how our language is peppered with all these expressions. You won't find them in textbooks. This is verbal language. Take pity on foreigners and try to speak English.

Now I want to turn to the subject of networking. I'm not talking about computers, I'm talking about people helping people. So many times we can be used in a small way towards solving a

The Soup of Life

problem. I always say, "I don't know much, but I know a lot of people who do." That's networking.

Now I want to tell you about a book I'm reading that is giving me joy and peace. *It's called A Day's Journey*, by Jon Courson. He sees things so differently and in a beautiful way.

Let me give you an example: he tells the story that in the Old Testament; sin was atoned by sacrificing a lamb. Now here's the interesting part. Priests spent hours examining the lamb to make sure it had no blemishes. The lamb was examined, not the person. I've never heard of this before in my life! What insight!

He says when you see misery, that's an opportunity for ministry. How concise, how wise, how true! I am so impressed with this man I'd like to try an experiment. I'd like to have a study based on this book. It's based on the Bible. I'd like to invite anyone who is interested to meet with me one hour a week. I don't care what church you go to, if you don't go to any church, or if you are male or female, young or old. The realm of thought excites me. New concepts are treasures. I hope so many of you will respond that we'll need a hall! Please call me at 679- 4772. We'll find a time and a place. Just so I don't have to feed all of you. Food, that is.

Margaret Valone

RELIGION

Introduction to Religious Holidays

Anyone who reads my columns knows that I am a born-again Christian and that my faith is very central in my life. For those who are not familiar with my religious history here is a short summary.

In March of 1978, I discovered at the Cleveland Clinic that I was born with a hole in my heart. The doctors gave me a 97 percent chance of having it repaired successfully. Those are good odds and my husband and I decided to go for it. Our first son, Rusty, was living in Miami, so I decided to fly to Miami where he and his wife, Barbara, lived along with their two daughters. The older was three and the younger, 16 months. I knew I had to give Rusty this news in person, so that he could see I looked the same and everything was under control. When he picked me up at the airport, he was all excited. "Mom, I'm a born-again Christian." It sounded nice, but I didn't know what he was talking about. He was surprised because I was always very religious and he took it for granted that I was born again.

He explained to me that during the Jews' captivity in Egypt, the Jews were treated so badly by Pharaoh that the Lord was going to punish him by taking the life of the firstborn in every household. The Jews would be spared by taking the blood of a perfect lamb and putting the blood on the door posts. Every house that had the blood of the lamb, the Angel of Death would pass over it. That is what the Jewish celebration is all about. Now Jesus is our perfect lamb and if we place ourselves under His blood, we will be spared a spiritual death. I had never heard this story before and I promised Rusty I would think about it. But I went home and put all my

The Soup of Life

thoughts on my upcoming surgery on May 23rd.

On Thursday evening, May 4th, I found out my sister had received a call that Rusty had been electrocuted at work. The shock, the sense of loss, the loss of future dreams we shared - all came pelting through my brain. The next day I received a call from someone in Miami, and this person told me that when Rusty died, two of his working buddies got down on their knees and surrendered their lives to Christ because they wanted to be like Rusty. One of them had been involved with gangster activities.

All of a sudden, I understood. God in His wisdom knew that death is a motivator. If our son's death could move those two young men, He knew His Son's death could move the world!

Rusty's body arrived and funeral arrangements were made. On Saturday evening, I went to bed. For some reason I awoke and went downstairs. I knelt at the toilet bowl and cried into the toilet, "Lord, I'm not worth flushing down this toilet. My sin is one of pride. I give it all up!" I had, considered myself an intellectual and I didn't want to be taken in. I had to learn that if I were not taken in, I would be left out. I went back to bed, fell asleep and woke up with prickling sensations running up and down my body! I realized I had received the Holy Spirit. Up until that time, I didn't know who the Holy Spirit was.

I was not the only one whose life was changed. Some of our employees were saved. One of Rusty's pallbearers had a conversion experience. And it grew and grew. One day my minister said, "I look at this congregation and three-quarters of them have come either directly or indirectly from your son's death."

Sometimes I could feel rather guilty that it took two sons to die for my life – first, God's Son and second, our son. But I remember once Rusty said to me, "If there's a situation that needs a volunteer - there could be 1,000 guys and I'd feel it's up to me to step forward."

So, I know that if God had said to him, "Rusty, your mom is a tough case, but here's my plan. Will you do it?" Rusty would have said, "Let's go for it." I was given a precious gift at great cost. With this gift came responsibility. I must use my gift of life with laughter, joy, courage, wisdom and sharing.

This is why I have to tell my story in hopes that it will affect you in a positive way.

Jesus Is the Reason for the Season

Merry Christmas!

Don't you just love Christmas? I do. Did you ever stop to think that Christmas brings out the best in us because Jesus was born to take care of the worst in us? Did you ever stop to imagine what kind of a world this would be if Jesus had never been born? Even those who don't believe in His deity will admit he is a good influence. I had some good Muslim friends who loved Jesus as a good prophet. What he taught influenced the whole world.

Let's start at the beginning. Who was Jesus and why did He have to born? When God created the world, it was so beautiful that He decided to create a man and woman to populate this beautiful world. Great idea, right? But what did man do? Why is it we can never stand prosperity? We have to spoil everything! That's what humanity did. They became greedy, mean, spiteful, corrupt, etc. They became so bad God repented that he had created them. Something had to be done to correct this situation. He would send his Son down to earth. He would be born of a virgin and his father would be God, the Holy Spirit. He had to be God so that he could not sin. Then he had to be human so that he could die. He was one of us and yet he was above all of us. The beauty part of this story is that Jesus was made aware of his future and all the pain it entailed and he agreed to be our substitute because it was the only hope for us. Now that's what I call love!

Christmas is the beautiful part of his life. Easter is the painful part of his life. Now let's look at his life. He started out as the son of Mary and Joseph. I always feel we don't give Joseph enough honor for the part he played in Jesus' life. How many men would stick by a woman who looked like she was having another man's baby? Not everyone heard the voice of the Lord telling Joseph that this baby was the son of God. Going beyond that, how many would believe it? But, Joseph was a believer and he was a good father in every way. They lived simply. He was a carpenter and he taught his son well.

Let's examine Jesus' friends. John the Baptist, was his cousin and also the forerunner of Jesus' work. Then there were the 12 disciples who were to be his couriers. Jesus was their teacher. What did he teach them? He taught them first of all to be humble. What are some of the signs of humility? He never talked about his power or made people aware of how powerful he really was. He came to earth as a modest carpenter. He wasn't born into a rich family. He wasn't a politician with a lot of clout. He never swaggered or bragged. On the contrary, He was kind, loving, merciful, patient, yielding, compassionate, giving and forgiving, peaceful, etc. He never retaliated when people wronged him. He was a holy man. He was and is our example. He could have felt justified to turn on his accusers and men that belittled him and hurt him, but he didn't. He turned the other cheek. I say the reason why most people can't turn the other cheek is because they are too stiff necked! They lack humility because they have been conditioned to be proud.

We can all make this Christmas an extra good memory if we concentrate more on being more like Jesus every day of our lives. We could learn a lot by looking at the things Jesus didn't do. We never saw him a gamble or cheat. We never saw him do drugs or get drunk. We never saw him steal or beat someone up. We never saw him put someone down, either physically or verbally. We can go on and on. Life is a combination of things we do and things we don't do.

Examine yourself and see how you can be more like Jesus. That is showing real love. The biggest compliment you can give anyone is imitating him. Let's be more like Jesus and that will be a Merry Christmas and a merry life. Here's a poem I wrote. I'm not a poet. I wrote this with all humility. Please look at the message, not the form.

The Soup of Life

A Christmas Poem
Today is the 25th of December.
This date makes us remember.
What life is all about.
Jesus taught us the most important thing is love.
If we have an abundance with joy we should shout.
So how did we learn about love?
It came to us all from heaven above. It was the birth of this Savior.
That taught us His love.
His love was sacrificial and unconditional.
It was sweet and pure.
If we accept it
We will know for sure
That we are His forever more.

Merry Christmas, Everyone

I don't think I've ever had more Christmas spirit as I have this year. First of all, I'm more aware of the purpose of the birth of Jesus and something new has happened. Someone is putting a gift behind my door every day for the 12 days of Christmas. The first day I found a poinsettia plant and I said, "Oh, how nice." The second day it was a box of spaghetti and a small bottle of ice wine. I have never heard of ice wine before, but my son tells me it's expensive. On the third, I found three hot chocolate envelopes; the fourth, four chocolate candy bars; the fifth, five candles; the sixth, Life Savers; on the seventh, there were seven pencils; and on the eighth there were cookies. That's all so far.

I'm getting teased about having a secret admirer. My answer is "If I do, he sure knows how to keep a secret!"

I have a special treat for you. I was fortunate enough to receive Mike Loomis's poem on the *'Twas the Night Before Christmas*. He said I could share it with you. Here it is:

> 'Twas the night before Christmas, all of heaven's abuzz
> Starting tomorrow nothing's as it once was,
> God came to earth to be born in a manger,
> Our alienation from Him had put us in danger.
> All went about as things were before
> Not realizing that God had just opened the door.
> Few were aware of what would happen this Day
> Known only to those who knew how to pray.
> The One who had come, to save us from sin

The Soup of Life

Was born in a stable, no room in the inn.
That's how God did it, without great display
Our Lord, and our Savior asleep on the hay.
The shepherds and magi, they came for a visit
The stable surroundings were hardly exquisite.
The stench of the animals, and smell of manure
This Kingly place seemed too demure.
But that's how He chose it, it was not inane
He came to earth, that He might know our pain.
Life is not easy, we all know that's true
That's why He came, for me and for you.
All through the Scripture the event was foretold
From early in Genesis to the prophets of old
From Ezekiel, Zechariah, and especially Isaiah
They wrote of the One who would be the Way.
He came to us, as Rome ruled the earth
Where only the elite had any worth
He would one day, share with us God's view
To take away sorrow and to make our lives new.
He would grow up to know He's God's Son
To understand there was work to be done
He spent time in Church and time on His knees
For it was only his Father he wanted to please.
Then He gathered about Him a small group of guys
Nothing to look at and not very wise
So they did follow to near and afar
And went everywhere without plane, train or car.
And as this One spoke, it was like nothing they'd heard
And despite opposition He was not deterred
He spoke of His Father as if He's a friend
Who despite all our sin,
His love has no end.
But none understood His work was not done
For the freedom of souls had yet to be won
So all of our sin He took to the cross
And all of His followers felt a great loss.
Don't cry or fret, it's not the end of the story
Christ would arise, so to God be the glory
That babe in the manger had finished God's plan

And now the way of salvation was open to man.
As people believed their hearts were set free
Their eyes were once blinded but now they could see
Their fear, hate, and worry He would replace
With his peace, love, and joy, understanding, and grace.
So as you retire on this Christmas Eve
Know all that He asks is that you believe
And now hear His voice without any fright
'Happy Christmas to all, and to all a good night'

Now I have my final thoughts for this Christmas. There's so much I can say about the meaning of Christmas and why it was necessary for Jesus to be born. We know he was born to take away the sins of the world for all who believed in him. In order to do this he had to be sinless. All men and women sin. So he had to be God to be sinless and since God can't die, he had to become human (man) so that he could die. We must not forget Mary conceived him through the Holy Spirit who still remains as a teacher.

Jesus was the one who was eligible to be our sacrifice. He loved us so much he accepted the sacrifice. It was all put in motion on Christmas. Christmas is our future. It could be a good life on earth or it can expand to eternity. I find all of this very exciting. So I really am merry. I wish you all the same. We can't be perfect, but we can be cheerful and thoughtful!

Jesus Gives Us Second Chances

How the time flies by! We're getting closer and closer to Christmas. Let's look at the word "Christmas". The first six letters spell "Christ". That is only fitting, since it reminds us that this is Christ's birthday. And we can spell "mass" with two s's because we'll have a mass of joy, laughter, love, and presents for those we love. We'll be busy planning a big party. The Christmas tree is a big part of Christmas. All the lights on the tree and around the windows remind us that Jesus is the light of the world! Everyone loves light and is either afraid of the dark or just doesn't like it. We can choose the light.

Have you ever asked yourself, "Why did Jesus have to be born?" We'll look at the big things first and then the smaller things. First of all, He had to be human. As a human being, He could feel pain, He could laugh, He could get angry, He could give love and be loved. He showed concern for others. Look at how He fed thousands with five fish, He encouraged people, He brought some back to life (Lazarus). He walked on water.

He had to be human so that He could die. And He had to be sinless so that He could be worthy of being a perfect sacrifice to remove our sins. He had to be a king. He had to fill all the requirements He needed to be the perfect sacrifice.

Now let's take a look at Mary. What was required of her to be eligible to be the mother of Jesus? She was a woman of virtue. She was willing to take the ridicule she would have to receive by being pregnant without a husband. But she stood up tall and met all the requirements.

And what about Joseph? Just think of the price he had to pay! Who would believe Mary got pregnant without being with a man? It looked like Mary had made a fool of him. And we all know how man is proud by nature. But he believed God when God told him in a dream that Mary was still a virgin.

Here was this beautiful family - different from any other. Mary, a mother without sexual experience; Joseph, a father without sexual contact; and a beautiful baby boy whose father was God. It took great courage for each one to do his or her part. Yet it was all done for the love of us.

I used to think God wasn't fair to Jesus for making Him suffer and die like that, but then one day I saw the light. Both of them put us first! Our needs came first! Wow! That's what I call love! I didn't see it because I wouldn't do that.

Why should I allow my son to suffer and die to save those people? Besides - they were bad people. They were sinners! I could understand more if they were at least good people. That's why I couldn't get it. But you know something? When I hear those stories of how people have changed their lives because of the love of God and Jesus, I find myself most impressed by those who were really bad and completely changed. If you had been a prostitute or a promiscuous woman and you gave it all up because you were sorry and you appreciated the sacrifice Jesus had made for you, that's more dramatic than a girl who was telling lies and stopped that bad habit because she didn't like herself anymore.

I know of a woman whose husband had lied to her and cheated on her. She decided to be worse than he was. She did everything he had done and more to pay him back. Do we do stupid things like that? Do two wrongs make a right?

Fortunately, someone saw her plight and rescued her. She became a teacher, and an excellent one at that. Don't ever think you're too bad to be saved. No one isn't good enough to be worth saving. We're all sinners, but let's hope Christians sin less. We're better than we were, but not perfect.

I know another young man - he used to smoke, drink, do drugs.

The Soup of Life

You name it, he did it. He turned his life completely around! He's such a beautiful Christian! I love his story. Maybe I'll ask him for permission to write his whole story. It would be such an inspiration.

I count my blessings every day. I thank God for this column. I'm not professional (except for being a hairdresser). I'm just an ordinary person, but maybe that's why people relate to me. Sometimes professional people intimidate others. A thought just came to me - do you think that's why Jesus left off being a king and became just an ordinary person? He's the wisest person I've ever met, so I bet that's what He did! I'm appreciating the real meaning of Christmas more and more every day! This is going to be a special Christmas! Merry Christmas!

Margaret Valone

Celebrating the Spirit of the Season

Every Christmas I try to see new meaning, deeper meaning in the Christmas story. Today we're going to look at it as the beginning of God's master plan.

The Bible tells us that man had become so sinful, God repented that He had made man. You see, God is a Holy God and a just God. He hates sin and a price has to be paid for sin. This is just. Justice is giving people what they deserve, whether it is good or bad. Now the sins of the world were so bad, a big price had to be paid. Who could be eligible?

Now the master plan begins. He would have a son who would be part God to be able to remain sinless. No human being could ever fulfill that requirement. And He would be human too so that he could feel the human frailties and be able to die. What am I saying? A father creates a son to die? How can this be? On top of it all, He was going to die for sinful people? They weren't even good people!

The Bible tells us in John 3:16, "For God so loved the world He gave His only begotten Son so that whosoever would believe in Him would not perish, but have everlasting life." There's the answer. "For God so loved the world." He loved us so much. He put our needs ahead of His Son's pain and suffering. When I think of this as a parent, I can't imagine such love! I couldn't do it for sure. And you men out there, could you do that to your son? Incredible! We can look at the loss and the pain or we can look at the gain. The gates of heaven were opened for us! We didn't open the gates with our good works, but we can show appreciation by following up this gift with good works, no matter how big or how small.

Now let's look at the Son.

He was to be born of a woman in the town of Bethlehem. Do you know that Bethlehem means "house of bread"? How perfect! Jesus, who was to become the bread of life, was born in the "house of bread"! His stepfather, Joseph, was a carpenter. The word translated as carpenter was "tekton". It means a finish carpenter rather than a framer. Joseph specialized in making yokes. The yokes were to accommodate lead ox with one that would follow. The lead ox pulled the greater weight. That's why Jesus invites us to yoke with Him. He will lead us. What a practical application.

Why do you think Jesus was born in a cave or manger? The King of Kings should have been born in a palace! No, this Godly man wanted to teach us to be humble, not proud. Have you ever had the experience that a product you normally bought had the packaging changed, so you couldn't find it? That's the story of Jesus. He didn't come with the expected packaging. The Jews wanted a leader to free them from the bondage of being under the Romans. They were thinking in the physical, while Jesus came to take care of the spiritual. Jesus knew from the beginning what His role was to be. He accepted this sacrifice because He loved us so much! Here are two acts of His amazing love. While He was hanging on the cross, He said, "Father, forgive them. They know not what they do." Imagine! Then He was not through with us, He sends us a gift - the gift of the Holy Spirit, who is with us today as our teacher and guide.

This is the most beautiful love story the world has ever known and it all began with Christmas. I pray my thoughts have given you a better understanding and appreciation of Jesus. If it has, will you show your love for Him in love for others? He asked us to love God with all our minds, hearts and soul and our neighbors as ourselves.

Before closing, I want you to think about three words. The first one is justice. I already talked about justice. It's giving us what we deserve. The second is mercy. With mercy we don't get what we deserve. The third word is grace. With grace, we get benefits we didn't earn and don't deserve. Jesus is our justice. And He has given us mercy and grace. The gift of eternal life is your Christmas gift from Jesus. Open it, accept it, and change your life.

Merry Christmas!

Pondering the Meaning of Christmas

Today is Christmas. Merry Christmas to all. It's a very special day and each one of us can make it special in our own ways. Of course, in essence it's a religious holiday, but in reality to most people it's just a holiday. Will everyone in your household give a Christmas blessing at the dinner table or will they just say something like "dig in"?

Everything is what you make it. This day is an opportunity to make things happen that will direct your lives. Who is this baby Jesus? How does His life affect ours? There are readers out there with different beliefs and different degrees of understanding, but that changes us, not Jesus. He never changes. He's always who He is. What did He teach His followers and his disciples? In chapter 5 of Matthew, He addressed the multitudes. I've just picked out a few. Jesus blesses the humble, the poor, the meek, the merciful, the peacemakers and those that seek out righteousness. All these positions concentrate on doing for others, thinking of their needs as well as our own. After all, we all have the same needs whether we're rich or poor.

Now these principles, when put into action, make better lives for all of us. What was so different about Jesus? After all, He was royalty. Why didn't He come as a king or at least a rich man? Let's consider that. How many people could or would relate to Him? Not too many. It was the poor and uneducated that were the majority and needed the most help. We always said, "The Lord helps the needy and not the greedy". Let's think of a few other principles. He taught "love your neighbor as yourself". That says a whole lot. Who is your neighbor? Actually, anyone you come into contact with. Not all people need money or services, but everyone can use a warm greeting such as a broad smile or a handshake. If your relationship is strong, even a hug is acceptable. I'm not a kisser, but use your discretion on that one.

Jesus also said, "Honor thy father and thy mother". Why? Because it shows respect and really pays off. He also makes you a promise if you honor your parents, you will be blessed with a long life. So that's why I'm still here! I think of my parents so often and am so grateful for the values they taught us! I strongly urge everyone, especially if you don't believe in religion, to study the Ten Commandments. They are all good principles to live by. Your life will be so much richer. Your relationships will be stronger and more rewarding.

To those who consider themselves Christians, I recommend you think of Christmas as the birth, the life, the death and resurrection of Jesus. This way we honor all of Him and it will change our lives. Just consider this. God made the greatest sacrifice a parent can make by giving up his son. Jesus made the greatest sacrifice He could make by giving up His life and leaving us the Holy Spirit to teach us. This is the greatest love story the world has ever known. Think about this, if you accept this message and when you die there is nothing there, what have you lost? But if you reject the message and I'm right, what have you lost? Think about it.

Have a blessed Christmas!

The Soup of Life

Dreaming of a White Street Christmas

I'd like to reflect on a Christmas past. The most memorable Christmas of my life.

The year was 1977. That year Russ and I decided to send money to our son Rusty's family for all four of them to fly north for Christmas instead of our flying south to Florida. This new arrangement would give his family an opportunity to visit all the cousins and friends back home. They were thrilled because he and Barb wanted the girls (their daughter Charlene, who was three-and-a-half, and Lori, who was one-year-old) to see a white Christmas. I was excited because I had bought a keyboard for them. Barb is an excellent piano player and I knew she would teach the girls to play as soon as they were old enough. Well, they all came and we had no snow. Then in the early evening huge flakes started to fall. Before long the streets were covered with a deep layer of fluffy snow. Someone had given us an old-fashioned sleigh. It was like a pram, but instead of wheels, it had beautifully curved runners for use in the snow. We got the girls all bundled up. Charlene was hanging on to Lori in the sleigh. Rusty and Dan were the horses. They started to pull the sleigh up and down White Street. There were big snow flakes falling in the street lights, rosy-red cheeks on the kids. It was like something out of a movie.

After the girls were home and in their normal clothes, Santa came to call with presents. Luckily, we had a Santa suit, one-size-fits-all. And Nin St. George played the part beautifully. He sat each girl on his knee and gave them their presents. They were so excited. They got to open up all their gifts because we do that on Christmas Eve. It was beautiful. Then Rusty and Barb sat at the keyboard. She played Christmas songs and we sang. Rusty looked up at me and said, "Mom, how can we ever top this Christmas?" Well, we never did. On May 4, 1978, Rusty was electrocuted at work.

I will always be grateful for this beautiful memory we were given that will last as long as any of us will live. Thank you, Jesus, for this precious gift.

Living in the Presence of God

Did you have a good Easter? I had an outstanding Easter! First, I had an unexpected guest. A good friend of mine called and said her husband came home with a serviceman who had formerly been a Baptist minister in Alabama. She asked if I would take him to church. I was delighted. Are you ready for this? His name was Billy Ray Robinson. Nobody will forget his name.

Next, our service had a young preacher from North East, PA by the name of Nathan Elliot giving the message. I am so impressed by these young men in their twenties who can really preach and have so much wisdom and maturity! In his message, he said, "Jesus intercepted" for us.

Suddenly, I saw God, The Father, as a quarterback who was hurling a football of death and sin to the wicked world. Suddenly, Jesus intercepted the ball, took on the death and sin meant for us and saved us. Then I saw that every time someone understands, believes in Him and accepts, Jesus makes a touchdown. Do you suppose I saw all this because I'm such a fan of the Buffalo Bills? Maybe other football enthusiasts would understand the role of Jesus better through this analogy. It really blessed me.

Later in the day, I saw a moth in the bathroom. I hate moths! Every time I see one I visualize holes in my clothes. I shut the bathroom door and said to the moth, "You're not going to leave this room alive!" Then I went after it with a vengeance. As Paul Harvey says, "Now you know the rest of the story." After it was over, I felt sorry for the moth. I saw people as the moth and the bathroom as the world. Nobody is going to leave this world without dying a physical death. It makes you stop and think what you want to do with your life.

Then last week I became aware of how few people know next to nothing about the last book in the Bible called "Revelations." Isn't it strange that the gospel of John is the best known and most read of all the gospels and yet the book of Revelations, which is also written by John when he was in exile on the Island of Patmos, is the least read? How do we explain this?

Well, the first tells about the past. The last tells about the future, which some day will be the present, too. Shouldn't we be interested in our futures? Do you know that everything Isaiah predicted about Jesus came true 700 years after his predictions? No one will know when the predictions in Revelations will come true, but they will. I've heard a Jewish scholar and preacher say we are definitely in the end times. There are many people and religious leaders who believe this is true. We are told that in the changes in the weather, many earthquakes, etc. Look at what's happening in Indonesia, Thailand, Burma, etc., all over the world.

If you want to know more, be sure to see the *Left Behind* movie series. You will learn about the rapture, the mark of the beast - 666, and many other things you may be vague about. Not all scholars agree on when the rapture will take place. It will be either before the seven years of tribulation or in the middle, or at the end, but they all agree it will happen. You can decide for yourself, but certainly now is the time to prepare.

The Soup of Life

Easter Musings

This column gives me a chance to tell some of my Easter stories and my thoughts about Easter. I attended the Easter service in 1987 in a church on the grounds of Cleveland Clinic. Don't ask me what denomination because I have no idea. All I know is it was beautiful! They sang *Wounded for Me* like I had never heard before. I happened to be there because my husband was a patient. He was going to be operated on his lungs. He had a roommate who had been very true to the Lord until he slipped and was living with a woman. We talked a lot and he said when he got out he was going to get married. He was a very nice man.

After Russ's operation, the doctors felt his room should be private and they moved his roommate. A few days later he came running over to see me. He was all excited with worry over his new roommate. He said I had to go over and witness to him. I did. I asked him if anything should go wrong what did he think would happen to him? He smiled with confidence and said, "I'm OK. I've never cheated on my wife, I'm a good father and I have a dry cleaning business and I've always been a good provider."

I responded, "Then Jesus was a fool to die for you." He replied, "What do you mean?"

"Well, you don't need him. You're going to heaven for all the good things you're doing. It's what you do, not what Jesus did."

"I'm confused", he said.

"Well let's put it this way," I explained, "let's say you were God. You created the world and it was so beautiful you decided to create

Adam, and later Eve, to let them and all who followed to enjoy your creation. Instead of being grateful they became hateful. They were so bad you were even sorry you created them! But you decided to give them a second chance. You would send your son down to bring them back to righteousness. Instead of following him, they persecuted him, beat him up, crowned him with thorns, laughed at him and nailed him to a cross where he died. Then one of the soldiers pierced him with his sword. What would you do?"

Without hesitation he answered in an angry voice, "I'd tell them to go to hell!"

And I replied, "So does God."

He couldn't have given me a better line to answer.

Then we talked. I told him he was lucky because he still had a chance to turn his priorities around and put Jesus first. He wasn't the only good person that has and is still doing the same thing. We have to remember that Jesus died for all, even though they were sinners. He didn't say you have to stop drinking or being promiscuous or a liar, a thief or a drunkard. No, it was nothing you had to stop doing. He didn't say you have to go to church every week or five times a day. You have to feed all the hungry, be a great provider or drive a great car to bring him honor - belong to the D.A.R., or Rotary, etc. It all comes from Him. He gets the credit and the glory. How do you feel when you do something nice for your family or relatives, or friends or church, etc.? And they show love and you receive love.

The greatest love of all is being a servant. Jesus said and showed it all. He became a servant to all of us. The only way we can show our gratitude is to become his servant in return and don't do it for credit. You will be rewarded in heaven. Just think of how good you feel when your children show you love and kindness. These are appreciated. On the other hand when they clutter, dirty the house, their friends come over and jump on the furniture, etc. do you throw your children out? Oh, you can throw the other children out, but you always keep your own. So it is with Jesus and His Father if you ask to be part of the family and tell them you accept their sacrifice. Then you will be under the blood of Jesus and He will be

The Soup of Life

your sacrificial lamb.

For 52 years, I would not accept the sacrifice Jesus made because it wasn't fair to Him. God, the Father, was all powerful. He could do what ever He wanted to. Why did He choose that way? It wasn't fair to Jesus.

I didn't understand until my son, Rusty, was electrocuted at work. He was a believer. Two of his friends got down on their knees and surrendered their lives because they wanted to be like Rusty. One of them was a hit man for the Mafia. He changed his life and countless others! Then I understood. Death is a motivator and a cruel death, an undeserving death, is a greater motivator. He died for us. What are we willing to do for him?

You can turn your life around this Easter. Great peace and joy await you. Accept the gift and put a big smile on your face.

Margaret Valone

Keeping the Faith This Easter

Tomorrow is Easter. Will this Easter be any different from all others? I hope so because life is a learning process. Every year I learn more about Jesus and my relationship to Him grows and grows.

I remember an experience years ago that changed my life. I went to confession and confessed that I was practicing birth control and I was going to continue to practice birth control because no one is good enough to go to heaven and I wasn't going to have more children to go to hell. The answer I got was, "We have to make sacrifices." What? Sacrifice my children? This was not a good answer. If he had said, "You're right. No one is good enough to go to heaven. That's why Jesus died for us. He was the only one good enough to take our place so that we can enter heaven through Him." I had to learn this later on.

We are by nature sinners. As I grow older, I see how selective we are about sin. Adultery is a sin. So are fornication, lying, stealing, murder, gossiping, being jealous of others, swearing, pride and many more. For some of these, we go to jail and others are ignored. If we went to jail for all of them, there would be no one left to run the country. Why do we tolerate some and punish others? Does number make it right? Like people who justify themselves by saying, "Everybody's doing it." Can we legislate morals? I don't think so. A decision to be moral comes from the heart, not the bench. It comes from the home, the church, and the schools. Being moral should be rewarding. Being immoral should be unthinkable.

The Soup of Life

If we understand the pain, penalty, and punishment Jesus went through for us, we should want to repay Him, by keeping His commandments and teachings. It's a heart behavior, not a social one.

This year because of Mel Gibson's movie, *The Passion of the Christ* the world is understanding the pain and sacrifice that Jesus made for us as never before. Some people thought that he should have shown the resurrection of Christ as the grand finale. I think he didn't do this because first impressions and last impressions stay with us. Therefore he would have defeated the purpose of making the events that led up to the crucifixion and the crucifixion itself, if he had showed the reward and the glory.

Now let's talk about the resurrection. This year let's think about it and appreciate it as never before.

The biggest difference between Christianity and all other religions is the resurrection. No other religion has a God that resurrected and lives. We serve a living savior. Because He lives, we too will live. That is our security. If you don't believe in the resurrection, you are not a Christian.

Recently, I was told there are two billion Christians in the world and one-and-a-half billion Muslims. Which one has the truth and how do you know? If you are depending on your intelligence to enlighten you, it will never happen. The Bible tells us we are saved by faith. If you have the proof, you don't need faith. But a funny thing happens, when you start with the faith, the proof follows.

Probably the most known chapter in the Bible is John 3. It is interesting to note that. Jesus says first that unless you are born again, you cannot see the kingdom of God. I think the word "see" means understand and accept because later He uses the word "enter" the kingdom of God.

In the great commission we are taught to go out and teach all nations, but it says nothing about punishing those who don't believe. We all have choices. If you're not satisfied with your choice, keep searching. If you are satisfied with your choice, then live it.

Margaret Valone

I hope this Easter will be the most meaningful Easter in your life so far. Keep growing.

Remembering the True Meaning of Easter

I do not use this column to force my religious beliefs, though, I try to use Christian principles that are good advice, common sense and universal, but these are nondenominational. However, tomorrow is Easter, the most important day in the Christian world. The story of the life of Jesus has a most unusual beginning and it has no end. Let us examine His life.

There has never been a birth like His. His father was God, the Holy Spirit, and His mother was a kindhearted young virgin who gave birth to Him. So in essence we are saying He was God, yet human. Why this combination? He had to be God to remain sinless and he had to be human to replace human sins. Why was this necessary? In the Old Testament we learn that the atonement for sin was a blood sacrifice. The animal had to be a perfect lamb, one without blemish. Now, Jesus is our perfect lamb. This is why we say, "Lamb of God who takes away the sins of the world". He was born to die for atonement of our sin. He knew this from the very beginning and He accepted the assignment. What perfect love!

All His life, He was the teacher, the rabbi. He taught people how to live the good life. He never owned a mansion, or a fancy chariot (He entered Jerusalem on a donkey), and He-never carried a suitcase. We could go on and on. He was a humble God, not proud.

We know that while He was on the Cross, He was taunted by men to come down from the cross if He was God. He saved others, but He couldn't save Himself. But he endured because it was necessary. He was the only one that could open the gates of

Heaven for all mankind. The only requirement was that they believe in His sacrifice, and accept His gift of salvation. Now we can't leave Him on the Cross. That was the end of His human-ness, but the beginning of His eternal God-life. All the credit for our salvation goes to Him.

Let us say you have led a good life. You have done so much good and you can put it all in your savings account to present it to the keeper of the heavenly gates. When you got there, your savings was refused. You could only enter on Jesus' credit card. Are you willing to give all the credit to Him? "What about all of my good works? Don't they count?" you ask.

Yes, of course they count. They have made you happy and they have made Christ very happy. However, they are not the keys to the kingdom. When you want the credit to count for getting you into heaven, you are denying the credit that should go to Jesus. His pain and shame and death did not count for you. You had to do it your way. Are you so proud that you really would do that to Jesus? Please, look up in your Bible Ephesians 2:8-9. It reads, "It is a gift of God: Not of works, lest any man should boast." I believe this is in all Bibles.

So you see, Easter is celebration of new life. Christ was the first to rise from the dead and all who believe will join Him. Easter is the greatest victory of all time.

- Happy Easter!

HOLIDAYS

New Year, New You

The new year, 2011, has just begun. What's so important about a new year? It's an opportunity to give our lives a new direction. That's great, but first we have to be motivated. I wish we could make proper changes out of love but most of the time our love isn't strong enough, so I'm going to try to use anger into today's column to motivate you.

People ask me, "Do you ever get mad? I always see you happy."

Are you kidding? I get very angry at injustice, stupidity, greed, lethargy, nonparticipation in all the things that affect our lives. For example, when I see illegal immigrants marching and protesting, I get mad because the legal citizens of this country aren't protesting. Am I against immigrants? Of course not. My family started as immigrants - legal immigrants. With our country being in the bad shape we're in, we cannot afford to feed them or keep them in jail. I feel sorry for them but we can't take responsibility for all the needy in the world. Come in legally and I'll welcome you.

Now that's one problem but do you want to know what and who is the big problem? Look in the mirror. Yes, we're the problem. Let's look at the government trying to eliminate some of the tax cuts the rich have been enjoying. The rich say, "I earned it. It's mine. Who are you to take it away?" They have a point. On the other hand, the poor at the other end of the spectrum many have run out of unemployment checks and have no income. They need help. Where is this help going to come from? You can't get much out of those who are barely making it on their own. It seems logical it should come from the people who have excessive income. How much does one need anyway?

It's not a question of need. It's a question of greed! Money brings power and all of this feeds the ego - pride. Wouldn't it be great if the wealthy would decide to help the needy? They could decide how much they would give, then let all the media report the donations and praise the biggest donors. Start a competition among them that would help provide the needs of those less fortunate. I'm dreaming, right? But you know, taking it on a lower level, how great do you feel when you help someone? Good deeds are their own rewards on earth. You have it in your power to make a great life for yourself by helping others.

Now let's look at the people who have little or less than the rich. Do you ever turn down a handout that is given to you? If you don't, you're no better than the rich man who won't share. I see HEAP urging people to apply for help with the heating bills. Many of these people can afford to pay their own bills but they take the handout. It's the same old thing on a lesser level. If you say to yourself, "Yes, but if I don't take it someone else will," then take it and give equal amounts to charity. Can you look at yourselves in the mirror?

Oh, how I wish our problems could be fixed through love. Love is sharing and caring, giving until it hurts. Examine yourself. Where are you on the scale of giving? Or maybe you're hoarding as much as you can for your future. I've got news for you. If you live long enough and lose your mind or your health - the doctors and the caregivers will bleed you dry. Be rational and save some, share some. What would Jesus do?

Now, I'm going to tell you a true story that will gladden your heart. When a friend of mine was 12 years old, a beggar came to the door. He asked for food. I'll call the boy Tim because he wants to remain anonymous. Tim invited him in and made a peanut butter and jelly sandwich. Before he could screw the bottle tops on again, the sandwich was gone. Tim made him another one and made an extra for the road. He also found his thermos, filled it with milk and gave it to the man.

The Soup of Life

Tim asked the man where he was going and the man said he was going to New York City. He had a good idea and he hoped his friends would finance him. Four years passed. One day a good-looking car came into the driveway. A well-dressed man came out. He knocked at the door. Tim answered it and the man asked, "Do you live here?"

"Yes," Tim answered.

"How long have you lived here?"

"Sixteen years."

"Do you remember the day a beggar came to your house and you gave him peanut butter sandwiches?"

"Yes, I do."

"Well, I'm that man. My idea was successful. Here's a thank-you check."

He handed Tim a check for $500!

Now this happened 40 years ago. Five hundred dollars was considered a lot of money and to a 16-year-old, it was a fortune!

Now this is the way life should work for all of us. First the young man had compassion for a needy person. Then later the rich man gave from his abundance.

Now, we have no control over the rich man, but we do have control over ourselves. Let's welcome every opportunity we have to help someone out. I hope we all have this heart condition. No, it doesn't need a doctor for repairs. These acts teach the heart to sing.

Make your own happy new year!

Margaret Valone

For the New Year, Take Some Inventory

It's getting to that time of year when we make our new year's resolutions. This is a new beginning. It's time to take inventory of what's going on in our lives. Let's continue to do the things that are working and improve on the things that are moderate to bad.

I'm going to use my body to remind me of the areas we need to concentrate on. Let's start with the mind.

What kind of thoughts have you had in your mind? Just remember that your thoughts precede your actions. Everything starts in the mind. Are your thoughts productive or destructive? Are they negative or positive? Let's think happy thoughts. Have you laughed a lot? Have you made others laugh? Don't forget, laughter is like medicine, so medicine goes into the mouth and comes out laughter. Great!

What else comes out of your mouth? The Bible tells us what is in our hearts comes out of our mouths. And it also says it's not what goes into the body that defiles it, but what comes out. Wow! That's a biggie! Let's see: did I give out more compliments than complaints? How about gossiping? We think of gossip as negatives being spread. This is an area that is so common that people accept it. If most people are doing wrong, that doesn't make it right. It might make our conscience feel better so we have to be aware of the truth of the matter.

Let's look at hospitality. Do you welcome people into your life? Do you invite them into your home? Do you try to comfort people with trials and worry? Are you an encourager or a discourager? Remember, praise costs nothing, but pays big dividends. Start with

The Soup of Life

your family. Your spouse and your children could use some praise. I'm sure you don't forget to tell them what you expect from them. We are competitive by nature, so if you give someone a compliment, he will want bigger compliments and more often. This is a good deal.

Now about finances? There are so many people who are out of work or as the price of things go up, what you're earning can't cover the cost of living. Actually, this can draw the family closer together. Have a family meeting and come out with things you can do to save money. Let the children be a part of solving the problem. Have you ever thought that good parents are teachers? Oh, you don't have any diplomas on the wall, but you're still a teacher. That is one of your talents. We all have talents - what are yours?

We've touched on hospitality, being encouragers, being a teacher and training your mind and your mouth. Be a good example. Ask yourself this: Am I an organizer or a follower? Both are needed. Are you a resource person and a networker? What are you good at? What gives you pleasure? These questions will lead you to good decisions for the new year.

This may sound like a serious column, but actually it is a happy column because it can direct your thoughts to outcomes that will bring you joy.

Happy New Year!

Margaret Valone

Happy Father's Day

When you think of the role of a father in the household, what comes to mind? I think of a father as the protector, the provider and the strength and the male role model. The father is very protective of his family. You'd better not do something nasty to anyone in his family or you'll have to answer to him. Everyone knows that so this makes his children feel secure and the offender feels threatened. The father keeps everyone in line.

Now let's look at the father as a provider. The weight of providing for the family falls on the shoulders of the father. You'll never know the heavy load that is until you have to carry it, I know because I played that role for a very short time. Let me tell you, it was scary. The father builds the house, the mother runs it. The father has to make heavy decisions. He has to use his head and she has to use her heart more. Although she does make the small everyday decisions, the father decides where you're going to live and how you're going to live. Of course, his wife has to cooperate, but he is the leader.

When we talk about his strength we not only mean his capabilities to lift and carry heavy objects, but his strength of character. I know my husband, Russ, said he would never ask our boys to do anything he wasn't willing to do and he kept his word. We all knew how to cook, clean, wash clothes and iron most things. In teaching them all these things, he was making good husband material for the boys. Our daughters-in-law really appreciate the many talents our boys had. By doing this he made good workers out of the boys. It wasn't a "guy thing" or a "girl thing". It was just taking responsibility when the occasion arose. In that way they learn to be good workers in many areas.

I always regretted we didn't have any daughters, because I know what a good role model Russ would have been to his girls. They would want to have husbands just like their father. I love to see little girls hanging onto their father's legs and looking up at them with adoring eyes. A father shows his boys what they should be and he shows his daughter what their husbands should be. In order to do all these things, the father has to play his role every day. It can't be hit and miss.

I don't know about you, but when I read the births in the newspaper, I look to see how many are married. It's frightening to think that many of these children will grow up without a father. And of course, the mother has no husband. Even if the mother is a good mother, she can't replace a father's influence. It takes both a good father and a good mother to make a healthy home.

Boys and men, think twice or more, before you have sex. This moment of pleasure can be very costly, not only in money, but in anguish. An ounce of prevention is worth a pound of cure. This bit of advice is my gift to you this Father's Day. Do things right and Father's Day will be priceless for you.

Now I'm going to tell you a good story and a funny story about an Italian immigrant father. He came to this country and opened up a restaurant. He was a very practical man. His bills that were due were on a spindle, food to be ordered notes were in a box under the counter and the cash was in the register. His son had just graduated from college as an economics major and knew all the latest business practices. He asked his father, "How can you possibly know how much profit you make?"

His father answered (you have to add the accent) "when I got off the boat I had nothing, but the pants I was wearing. Today your brother is a doctor, your sister is a teacher and you are an economics graduate. Your mother and I have a nice house in the city and a small farm in the country. We have a good business, a nice car and it's all paid for. You add that all up, subtract the pants and there's your profit."

Don't you love it? You can add up all the education, all the diplomas but it's common sense that wins out.

There, I hope I let you stick out your chest a bit, gave you some good examples and good advice and lastly, I made you laugh a lot. That does it for me. I hope it did it for you.

Happy Father's Day!

The Soup of Life

Sharing Your Love with Others Every Day

Sunday is Father's Day. The older I get, the more I realize the significance of the role the father plays in the lives of his children. Each child looks to his father as a provider and a protector. He is too young to say those words, but he feels safe when his dad is around and when he wants to buy something, Mommy should say, "We'll ask Dad to see if we can afford it."

This is a difficult time for some dads because they have lost their jobs. It's unfortunate that most men identify themselves by their work. Have you ever noticed when you ask a man to tell you about himself he'll begin by saying what he does for a living? Men, you are so much more than that! First of all, you're love. You bring much love to everyone in the home. Why do young children run to meet their dads, wrap their arms around his leg? When dad throws them up in the air, they never worry about falling - daddy is security, in more ways than one. Dad is also authority. He tells us what we can or cannot do. He reinforces what mom says. In a good family, the two of them will be of one accord. Along with feeding them, clothing them, and protecting them, he plays with them. Sports are good for both sons and daughters. Of course, you don't pitch as hard to a daughter as you do to a son, but you don't exclude them either. I look at Katie Bartkowiak and see what a fine baseball player she is and I remember what a good player her father, Rich, was. I never missed a game. He was in the outfield, and he could really hit a ball. I'm sure he and his wife Ann have encouraged Katie all the way. That's another role the father plays. He's an encourager. He gives praise at every opportunity. Whether he realizes it or not, he shows his children how to dress. When he comes home from work he'll take off his work clothes and put on something casual - play clothes - just as the kids should distinguish between school clothes and play clothes. Then on Sunday, he dresses in his best clothes to go to church. Whether he realizes it or not, he's showing and teaching respect. I've been trying to stay with "p" words like provider, protector, praise giver Therefore, instead of calling dad a teacher, I'll give him a promotion and make him a "professor".

When choosing a husband, a young girl looks for the fine manly characteristics her father has. Of course, this is only true if you are brought up in a healthy family where the mother is what a mother should be and a father is what a father should be. I think if we had to sum up a good father we can do it with two words, humble and loving. Humility is putting others first and you can do it because this action is done in love. It's so much easier if we have the original teacher in our lives. Whether you are religious or not, I think Jesus taught us all how to love. You can't do it through pride.

We've talked about ideal family, happy family. Unfortunately there are many homes without a father. This should not be. Many children feel abandoned and unloved. Boys react to this condition by joining gangs, getting into drugs and other crimes. Everyone needs to be loved. If you see a young boy who needs a connection, why not make yourself that connection?

If there are unwed fathers reading this column, make some changes in your life. You might start doing it for a child but you will be amazed at what it will do for you and to you. You can't give without receiving. And if you have a loving family, take in a child who has no such blessing. I don't mean adopting them, but allow them to be a friend. Let them see what they are missing so that they will want it for themselves. You can't want what you have never seen, but once you've seen it and want it you'll be a great father. Your children will love and respect you. That's another great word for fathers - respect. Respect is always followed with love. Being a father is one of God's greatest blessings. Make the most of it. You are appreciated!

A Father's Role

This column is dedicated to the role of fathers in households and those that should be in households.

Men, how do you see yourselves as husbands and fathers? The Bible says the man is the head of the household. It also says that you, men, should love your wives like Christ loved the church. Well, if you recall, the church is people and Christ died for them, so you should be willing to die for your wives. So you ladies out there who have griped about submitting to your husbands, just remember who got the better deal.

Now let's get back to the role of fathers. I want you to take a new course in three Rs. These Rs are Respect, Responsibility and Reasoning.

Respect starts with you. If you want respect, you have to give respect. Every good relationship starts with respect. Examine yourself. Do you demand more of your spouse and children than you are willing to give? If you don't want your children to swear or smoke or use alcohol at all or in excess, etc., do you apply these rules to yourself? Don't ever forget that you are a teacher and you teach best as an example.

Let's look at your relationship with your wife. Do you show love and affection? Oh, kissing her goodbye and hello are fine, but you show real love by sharing all the responsibilities in the home. Here's an area that is most important. You and your spouse should decide what kind of behavior you expect from the children, let the children know what the ground rules are and that the two of you agree on the punishments or rewards, and then stick to the program. I can't tell you how important this is. Don't give in unless circumstances demand it. If the children know you are serious, they will comply.

How are you going to enforce these rules? You certainly aren't going to hit them, but you can give them chores to do, like cleaning the dishes, sweeping and mopping the kitchen floor, cleaning the bathroom and so on. These are the things they can do as punishment and then have a list of things they can't do, like use the TV, only use the computer for homework, attend sports events for a week or two, no videos, etc.

Let's go back to what importance the family, the schools, churches, and governments have on our society. Sticking to that group, mom and dad - especially dad - have to emphasize respect for each other in the family; respect for teachers and administrators, respect for the clergy, and respect for men of authority in government. If they don't, they will get in serious trouble. If they do, they will have happy lives. Remember, for every action, there is a reaction. Showing respect is high on the list of good actions and reactions.

Fathers, I can't stress enough your role in the family. It has surprised me that children remember what their fathers say more than what their mothers say. One child told me the mother is always talking and it goes in one ear and out the other, but when the father speaks, he represents power and authority.

I don't want this column to be all serious.

How much fun does your family have on the whole? Do you communicate a lot? Do you eat at the same time? The dinner table can be a different kind of school. Do you plan fun activities? Picnics? Trips? Ball games? Backyard games?

We can't be all work and we can't be all play. Have diversity and a good balance. Please take this column seriously. We need you!

The Changing Role of the Father

This Sunday is Father's Day. I was thinking of how the image of a father has changed throughout the years. In the old days, the father was thought of as a disciplinarian with a strap in his hand or across his lap. It all depended on whether he wanted you to stand up or he put you across his knees. In those days, children obeyed their fathers. They were afraid of them. Some people say they were respected. Why is it that sometimes we interchange the words "respect" and "fear"? Either way, the children knew father, papa, or daddy was the head of the house.

It always amazed me when I heard men talking about the beatings they got, either with a smile on their faces or a look of respect. It never was with resentment. Do children really want discipline and respect it?

Later, the picture changed to, "All my father had to do was give me that look and I straightened up." So they went from a strap to a look. Then, later, it was a threat that never was carried out. Now it's "Go to your room!" As if that is a punishment. The young child probably has a TV, a computer, a cell phone, games, comic books, etc. Some punishment that is. You know, Dad, if you put a refrigerator in the room, you can lock him up for days.

If you have noticed, I have referred only to males. That's because I usually couple fathers and sons in my mind and I don't think fathers hit their daughters very much. A scolding would do the trick. And some girls learned how to wrap fathers around their little fingers at an early age and never lost the knack.

Let's look at the image of fathers today. We picture fathers playing ball with their sons or taking them to ball games, etc. They spend time on special occasions with their daughters, like going to school activities and, of course, walking them down the aisle and footing the bill for the whole thing. We should probably say "the hole thing." It's a lot cheaper to marry off sons.

Now let's look on the other side of the coin. How many males have provided sperm for children, but have never been fathers to them? Now, as never before, there is a large percentage of households with one parent - the mother. This situation causes many problems in our society, not to mention in the households themselves. The woman has to work and raise the children by herself. There is no father figure to direct the children and keep them in line. Men and women do not think alike. Therefore, they don't act alike. Children need both.

How many times, when we see both girls and boys being sent to jail, we see they are from one-parent homes? This is bad in so many ways. We usually think of how much it costs the taxpayers for welfare and incarceration. But what about the loss of a happy home and a normal lifestyle of achievement? It's everyday loving, caring and sharing, laughter and tears and comfort. How can we stop this cycle?

We call ourselves Christians, but I don't know of any church programs addressing all of these problems. If there are any, we need to know about them and get involved. Do other members of the father's family acknowledge these children? The family does not consist of the father alone. Step up to the plate and take responsibility.

I'm grateful to my father. Fortunately, my name was Leone, which means lion, so we all had to be brave and strong. Then he would talk about the importance of a good reputation. He said in the old country when a young man picked out a wife, he looked at the girl's family. The family reputation was worth more than money. I remember my father picking berries with us one day. I felt so bad for him because he was built like a general and he was a proud man, but he taught us as long as a job was honest, never be ashamed.

The Soup of Life

He taught us to have a heart for the poor. We never turned down a bum off the streets or from railroad cars. Just rather recently, a man told me my parents used to help support his family because his mother was a widow. My mother brought food. My father gave money. I'm not ashamed to say we didn't have much money. After all, if you have an abundance, how big a deal is it if you part with a small portion?

I think the best thing he gave us was a secure home because he loved my mother so much. He adored her. He used to call her a saint. I remember the day my mother had to go to the hospital to be treated for her asthma. I found him sitting in a rocker with tears running down his face. In those days, you only went to the hospital if you were dying. My last word to fathers is: love your wife. The combination will make a happy home for everyone to enjoy.

Margaret Valone

Gold Nuggets of Wisdom

Happy Mother's Day!

Tuesday, May 4, I was a guest speaker for a mother-daughter banquet at Stockton Community Church. It was my third invitation and I was honored. For some reason I pictured teenagers and their mothers, but almost all were adults. I had to change some of my speech. I wanted to show the young girls their mothers who are older couldn't go back to think like they think any more than they could think and act like their 2-year-old sibling. Then I pointed out it's necessary to teach the younger groups through the wisdom of the older group. We have to learn through communication. We must remember that a big part of communication is listening. It's an art we all have to learn. I told them I remember the first time I was a speaker and sang a solo, *There's Room At The Cross For You*. There's still room, but I can't sing anymore. I sound like Katherine Hepburn. I gave them a sample and they all laughed. Then I told them that I had learned the time of the dinner had been changed to after I spoke because so many times people left after eating, so I was keeping them hostage. They were great.

I shared with them some of the "gold nuggets" of truth and wisdom I have learned through my lifetime.
1. Never want something you can't afford.
2. Never look at people who have more than you and be envious.
3. Look at people who have less than you and count your blessings.
4. Share what you have. It will make you happier as well as the person who receives.

The Soup of Life

5. Learn to see criticism as opportunities to grow in character. Examine what is said. Then be honest. If it's true, be smart and change. Otherwise you stay like you are and be stupid. Which would you rather be? This is a battle between pride and humility. I want you all to discuss this thoroughly.
6. Use your natural gifts such as great personalities, a good mind, a healthy body - all your strengths.
7. Use your time wisely. Doing for others is more rewarding than being selfish.
8. Have a positive attitude. Smile and laugh a lot. Adults only laugh 8 to 12 times per day, while children laugh over 100 times!
9. Ideas produce energy! Energy is powerful!
10. You are powerful. You have the power of putting a smile on someone's face.
11. You have the power to make wise decisions.
12. Here's a rule to help you. Anytime, young and older, you ask yourself "Should I or shouldn't I", you have answered your own question. The answer is "No!"
13. Give people compliments and encouragement.
14. Be flexible. Don't be rigid in your mind, body, or schedule. Open your eyes!
15. Life is a celebration. Celebrate at every opportunity!
16. If you want someone to change, you must change first.
17. Body language speaks volumes.
18. In order to reach the goal you must start at the beginning. Don't be afraid to initiate (discuss).
19. No one can take away from you what you freely give. Be a cheerful giver.
20. Worry about the pennies; the dollars will grow.
21. You can make a million dollars, lose it and make it again.
22. Love is blind, but the neighbors aren't. How do you want people to see you?
23. If you eat more than you need, you'll weigh more than you want.
24. Lethargy creates obesity.
25. All you get out of life is relationships and memories.
26. Whatever the mind can conceive and the heart can believe the hands can achieve.

27. You're born alone and you die alone. What you do in between is either to yourself or for yourself.
28. Internal development will produce external changes.
29. You don't have to have money to be rich.
30. You don't have to be sexy to be a lover.
31. You don't have to have a classroom to be a teacher.
32. People are looking for the coming of the Lord and forget He is already here. Let's use Him and grow.

Lastly I told them May 4 is a very special day for me. Last night was the 32nd anniversary of our son Rusty's death. It was through this tragic accident I became a believer and my faith has steadily grown stronger. Many people have become believers through Rusty's story. I hope to pass it along.

Rusty gave me the best Mother's Day gift I could possibly have. Through his teaching I learned to accept the gift of eternal life. I'll share this story any time, any place.

May you have a memorable day!

The Soup of Life

Are You a Good Mother?

I thought I had missed Mother's Day. I was so relieved to find out it's the 11th, not May 4th. I was saying this to a couple of girls and one girl said, "I wouldn't miss Mother's Day at all. I hated my mother." You know, I just couldn't believe my ears. It got me to thinking. All mothers should examine themselves. Am I a good mother? What will my children remember about me? Did my family laugh a lot in the past? Are we still laughing? Did I teach my children how to take care of themselves or did I do everything for them and they never learned? Did I teach them to do for others and feel good about giving others a hand? Did I teach them to be sensitive to other people's needs? Did I teach them to be in touch with nature? Did they have an appreciation for sunsets, a gentle breeze, new fallen snow, or for birds in the area or for animals? Animals are not only pets. They teach their owners to love and take care of the needs of their pets. Were you such a clean freak that friends or animals were never allowed? How do you rate?

You might be thinking, "What kind of a Mother's Day message is this?" Well, I hope it's a happy one because if you are answering "yes" to all the positive questions and "no" to all the negative questions, this is good news because you have been a good mother. If you aren't sure or you definitely know you had wrong answers, then you have time to correct your mistakes and improve your relationship with your children. Be brave enough to ask them these questions and let them know you really care.

Maybe today you received flowers or candy or were taken out to dinner or something special as an act of appreciation. Those are all good gifts, but communication is the best gift and talk is affordable, unless it's long distance. Always keep the lines of communication open. It doesn't matter who calls whom.

I think it's wonderful that we have a special day for mothers and another for fathers. The family unit is the basis of our society. We should always strive to grow in our relationships. Mothers are very special.

One woman said she is sad because her mother is no longer with her. That's not the way to feel. Don't remember the loss. Remember the love, the good times, the memories. For some reason I remember my mother ironing clothes. A lot of times when she ironed I sat and we talked together. I used to love to hear the stories about the old country. Her father was light skinned and blue-eyed and her mother had brown eyes and high cheekbones. She took after her mother, although she had her father's nature. He was a just man and a comedian.

My mother was a fantastic story teller. She had a fabulous memory. She and my father had a store and she would tell him what to write down for the records. She never went to school. All her life she wanted an education. She told me that she couldn't go because she had to take care of her little brother. One day she left him in a field and went to school. Fortunately, nothing happened to him, but she never went to school again until she had to prepare for her citizenship papers. But both she and my father had a high regard for education and they swore that their children would be educated if they had to mortgage the house. Now I'll tell you how my father was devoted to my mother. When my mother was delivering my sister Rose (from Ricky's Boutique), the doctor was having a hard time delivering her because she had a broken leg. He told my father, "It's either your wife or the baby. I can't save them both." My father answered, "You save my wife. We can have more children, but I'll never find another woman like her." It was a marriage of love and respect.

A happy home has to have both.

The Soup of Life

Cherish Your Loved Ones Every Day

On Saturday morning, May 3, I was a speaker for the Free Methodist Church in Gowanda. What a great congregation!

I must tell you how this came about. Of course, many of my speaking engagements are happening because of this column. I received a call from Connie Williams with an invitation. Of course, I said yes. I've done mother-daughter brunches and banquets before. It is a wonderful opportunity to have a positive impact on a very important relationship.

After I hung up, I asked myself, "Where is Gowanda? I'll have to find out and then take a dry run." I didn't want to get lost or show up late. I hate to be introduced as "The late Mrs. Valone." Thanks to my friend Kathy Reynolds, I learned how to get to Gowanda. We got into town and there were two steeples on the left side. We checked out both. One was the United Methodist Church and the other was Free Methodist. I told Kathy, "It's probably the Free Methodist. That's a prophecy that they aren't going to pay me." We laughed. Sure enough it was the free one I never have a set fee. I don't want to exclude anyone who has no money. Then too, I leave it open. If they are rich, the sky's the limit!

Then I thought of things I could tell them. All I knew about Gowanda was a neighbor always screaming at her two boys, "You're driving me to Gowanda!" They were only 14 and 15. They didn't even have a license. Come to think of it, she didn't have a car! (I made this up.)

Margaret Valone

My brother Roddy told me this joke. A young man who was institutionalized in Gowanda was watching a farmer working outside the gate. What are you doing?" he asked the farmer. "Oh, I'm putting fertilizer on my strawberries." The young man answered in a confidential tone, "You should try to get in here. They put whipped cream on ours."

Then I talked about my mother. She was only 4'11", but we had to say she was 5 foot tall. My mother was "Mighty Mouse". She would lift up a 100-pound bag of flour. Sometimes she would bake bread, assorted pies and work all night. When 6 a.m. came around she got ready to go to work in the canning factory. She did all these things with a smile on her face and a song on her lips. Fortunately, singing off key is not inherited. I told them how my mother taught us that work is love in action. You show people you love them by doing things for them that makes them happy. In so doing, it makes you happy too. Work is very rewarding. She always rewarded us with great praise. That's how I became a workaholic. One day while I was giving a talk in Hornell, I wanted to say this. Instead I said, "I became an alcoholic". It was an accident, but they loved it.

My mother taught us about relationships. She said that whether there is peace or war in a home depends on the woman of the house. If you want to win all the time, people will learn to hate you. But if you put others first, they will love you and give even more than you would have asked for. Just remember, every time you win, someone else loses. Is winning worth it?

Another principle we were learning is that for every action there is a reaction. For example, work is a positive action that brings great rewards. But if you are sullen and lazy, no one will want you around, either at work or play. A happy face is always a welcome face. If you laugh a lot, people like to be near you. I remember when we had the beauty salon, people would stay after they were finished. I was afraid some day a federal man would walk in and tell me I had to charge entertainment tax. A happy face is a must for a successful business. On the other hand, if you are grumpy and show a bad temper, what kind of a business would you have? Forget it. Save your time and your money.

The Soup of Life

However, the good news is it's all up to you .You can choose whatever action you want! You'd be foolish to choose negative actions. Who wants a negative reaction? Isn't it great? Your happiness is in your own hands!

I've decided this is going to be my central theme when I talk to groups. Sometimes, I've come into contact with kids who come from dysfunctional homes. Now how can we expect them to have functional homes, if they have never seen one? We have to show them there is a choice. So it is with the thought process. We have to show that thinking positive and acting positive give positive reactions.

Just think of all the things I've told you about my mother. She was a philosopher, storyteller, a singer and a wonderful role model. All of this takes me back to another of my favorite sayings - "All we get out of life is relationships and memories."

Thanks for the memories, mamma.

May 4 marked the 25th anniversary of our son Rusty's death. We will not leave the column on a sad note. I must tell you about a movement my friends and have started. When someone tells you "Have a good day" you have to counter with "Have a good life". After all, you give good wishes for one day, that wish expires at the end of the day. "Have a good life" is a forever wish. Make sense?

Do you suppose we can get the Irish to give more than just "The top of the morning"?

Have a happy Mother's Day and a good life!

Margaret Valone

Happy Mother's Day!

I found this while I was cleaning out some of the things I had kept. I thought it would be appropriate for Mother's Day. It's called *Why Women Cry*.

>A little boy asked his mother, "Why are you crying?"
>"Because I'm a woman," she told him.
>"I don't understand," he said.
>His mom just hugged him and said, "And you never will."
>Later the little boy asked his father, "Why does mother seem to cry for no reason?"
>"All women cry for no reason," was all his dad could say.
>The little boy grew up and became a man, still wondering why women cry.
>Finally he put in a call to God. When God got on the phone, he asked, "God, why do women cry so easily?" God said, "When I made the woman she had to be special.
>I made her shoulders strong enough to carry the weight of the world, yet gentle enough to give comfort.
>I gave her an inner strength to endure childbirth and the rejection that many times comes from her children.
>I gave her a hardness that keeps her going when everyone else gives up and take care of her family, through sickness and-fatigue without complaining.
>I gave her sensitivity to love her children under any

The Soup of Life

and all circumstances even when her child has hurt her very badly.

I gave her strength to carry her husband through his faults and fashioned her from his rib to protect his heart.

I gave her wisdom to know that a good husband never hurts his wife, but sometimes tests her strengths and her resolve to stand beside him unfalteringly.

And finally I gave her a tear to shed. This is hers, exclusively to use whenever it is needed."

"You see my son," said God, "the beauty of a woman is not in the clothes she wears, the figure that she carries, or the way she combs her hair. The beauty of a woman must be seen in her eyes, because that is the doorway to her heart - the place where love resides."

The author is unknown, but I thought it was precious.

The role of women today has changed in many ways. More and more women are working. Many have executive positions, but the way she loves her husband and her children never changes. Notice the order I used? Many times I was criticized because I put my husband a first. My defense was, "A strong marriage is the best gift you can give your children."

Years after my boys were grown, psychiatrists agreed with me. I asked our sons if they ever felt neglected and they answered, "No way!"

One year when I was a speaker for unwed mothers, some of them told me they got pregnant because they wanted someone to love and love them back. Were they telling us that they had replaced love with sex? Boy, have we failed them. Now with so many mothers working they will have to make a special schedule where they interact with their children. I strongly recommend that you eat as many meals as possible together. It was at the dining room table that we learned to know what was going on in the world and to be politically savvy. Also, we learned to be mindful of people who had less than we had. All the railroad bums came to our house. They loved my mother's fresh bread. Mothers are giving creatures.

The White Inn has given me a Mother's Day gift. They are open for business. I was thrilled with the front page story in last Sunday's Observer on the White Inn. Now I must give you a personal view. I live in a house that was built for Isabel White. I have watched this evolution from day one as dumpster after dumpster was filled up and hauled away. Believe me when I tell you that the Gambinos have gone all out. We owe them big time. Fredonia wouldn't be Fredonia without the White Inn. The Gambinos' goal is to restore the White Inn to its former glory.

I'm going to go in on Mother's Day and make a reservation for me and my friends next week. If you'd like to see it and have no one to go with, call me and we'll get a bigger table. This is going to be a special Mother's Day. Make a special memory!

FOOD AND HEALTH

Putting the Perfect Spin on Pizza

I just had the most hilarious experience. I've been housebound for two and a half weeks with only a few emergency errands that I had to run. I'm going stir-crazy, so I decided to do something I have never done before. Believe it or not I had never made a pizza. Oh, I cook up a storm, but the only think I bake is box cakes.

Anyway, I had bought two envelopes of Betty Crocker crust mix for pizza. They were cheap at Aldi's and I thought it would be worth a try. I've had them home for months. Today I was so bored, I thought I'd try.

Then the hunt began for a topping. I had a can of tomato paste that I could use, but I had no mozzarella cheese, no salami or pepperoni. What could I substitute? Someone had brought me two red peppers today (thanks Val) and I had an onion. I sautéed these, opened up a can of olives, diced those up and I had Romano cheese. These would be my substitute for toppings. In the paste I added a can of water and then generously sprinkled black pepper, Italian seasoning, minced garlic and basil.

Now for the crust. All I had to do was add a half cup of warm water to the mix, stir it up until it made a ball. It was kind of sticky, so I went for some flour. I had about 3 tablespoons left. I'd use it sparingly. Then the real.problem presented itself. I couldn't find a rolling pin. What the heck was I going to do? Then the light came on. Use the long flashlight in the bottom drawer! I sprinkled flour on it, put my hand over the switch and started rolling. It worked! The light came on a couple times and I turned it off. Rolling pizza crust in the dark was more exciting!

Finally, I had the pizza all assembled and I put it in the oven. I was laughing all the while I put that pizza together. I wish I could have captured the devil in my eyes, maybe I should say "mischief". I love to improvise, OK? It's a challenge.

I like to be challenged. My husband and two sons and I used to sit around the kitchen table and say we should be a Peace Corps family. We never did it, but we could have.

I waited until the timer rang and took out my picture-perfect pizza. Would it taste any good? I found the pizza cutter and dived in. It was very tasty. I could see where I had been generous with the black pepper, but that gave it a tang. I wasn't too sure, so I took another piece. That was my excuse because I'm trying to cut down on carbs. My verdict is in. I liked it! Now I'll have to make another one with all the proper ingredients. Who knows, we might have pizza at the Sunday dinner?

The Secret's in the Sauce

You know how I love to save money and pass on all good news. Well, the other day I asked a cleaning lady if she knew how to get rid of small ants. She told me a pharmacist told her toothpaste does the trick. I thought, "That's easy. I'll try it." I did, but I guess my ants didn't have teeth because they didn't go for it. Or maybe I should have used Colgate. Anyway, I sprayed some Raid over it and between the two of them, it worked.

I like to throw in some history now and then. History was my favorite subject. It helps us to understand who we are and why. Then it motivates us to keep things going so we can make our present history better and lay a good foundation for our future history. Isn't that exciting? Let's grow!

I'd like to quote from a letter I received from Bill Schank in prison. He wrote, "I don't pray to get out of situations. I pray for God to get into them and teach me. God is in the business of raising spiritual giants and spiritual warriors. He's not in the business of raising spoiled brats and spoiled children."

I found his quotation very touching. No one is all good or all bad and we can change for the better. I learn from Bill.

I'm trying to empty out drawers to make room for Florida company. I came across a whole page on the Gioia family written in 1985 celebrating 75 years of pasta making. It's a fascinating story. The Gioia Macaroni Co. is one of the many claims Fredonia has for fame. Antonio Gioia made his first spaghetti in the year 1910. Everybody made their own macaroni at that time. Even my mother used to treat us to homemade macaroni every once in a while, but Antonio's spaghetti made a big hit with everyone who tasted it. He started his first factory in Fredonia on Union Street. In 1976, he sold a majority interest to a British company.

I remember in 1976 when I was chairman of the Bicentennial Celebration. I contacted the Gioia Brothers. They came down and gave us spaghetti and sauce for our spaghetti dinner event. It was held at the Methodist Church. With all that cooperation, the dinner was a great success!

The original Gioia Macaroni Factory was founded by Antonio and Alfred Gioia plus Phillip Bellanca. Phillip was a fine mechanic so I suppose this talent helped with keeping the factory running. He lasted as co-owner for one year and then the factory name was changed to the Gioia Brothers Macaroni Factory.

Before we go any further, let's do a little history. We must start with Oragio Gioia who was married to Josephine DeCarlo. They had four sons: Antonio, Alfred, Louis, and Sam. They first lived on Water Street (Joy Town). I am assuming that they moved there because my uncle John Joy, who was married to my father's sister, was the first Gioia to emigrate from Valledolmo, Italy. Then the rest followed. They were hard-working people with hearts as big as all outdoors. Our mayor, Russell Joy, was the son of Chas Joy. They left their mark on the history of Fredonia too.

In 1985 the current president was Paul P. Luchsinger, but he was assisted by four of Antonio's grandsons. At that time the company had three varieties of spaghetti sauces, a pizza sauce, and 75 different shapes and sizes of pasta in 300 boxes.

The Gioia family always credited their success to their father's recipe. They use the finest semolina. Pure semolina is very yellow and milled from hard winter durum wheat. This is mixed with water. Eggs are added for the noodles. With this recipe, the Gioias have received awards of pasta in the Italy Food Fair in Rome several times. The Gioias always kept the quality of their macaroni. They didn't look for short cuts to make more money. They kept their integrity.

Body, Mind and Spirit

I hope I have good news for you. The mind is a storehouse. I'm going to try to give you bits and pieces of information that you can store in your storehouse. Then when you need it, you can tap into it and have a better life.

This information came from USDA's Beltsville Center in Maryland.

Doctors estimate that every time you reduce your cholesterol one percent, your risk of heart disease is lowered by 10 percent. If you lower your cholesterol by 20 percent, you will reduce the risk of heart disease by 60 percent.

Did you know that pectin lowers your cholesterol? It traps cholesterol and pulls it out of your body. Because pectin dissolves into a gel, it traps molecules of fat and cholesterol in your gut (doctor's word, not mine) before they can get digested. Since pectin itself isn't absorbed, it goes out of the body, taking all that fat and cholesterol with it. Pectin also disrupts cholesterol production in your liver. It also lowers insulin resistance. This can be a serious health threat to those who have diabetes, obesity and heart disease. Pectin even helps you to lose weight. It gives you that feeling of fullness so you don't eat so much.

Here's a great tip in the morning: slash your cholesterol by sprinkling cinnamon on your coffee, toast, or Quaker Oats. A half a teaspoon each day could cut your triglycerides and total cholesterol by 12 to 30 percent. I'm doing it. At the same time it boosts your body's ability to store blood sugar.

Oatmeal lowers your cholesterol and helps you lose weight. Also scientists have discovered that oats contain natural compounds that are 50 percent more powerful than even vitamin E in reducing your risk of heart disease.

Here's more good news on how to fight heart disease: nuts, all kinds, fight heart disease. Some are better than others - like almonds and walnuts are better than peanuts. If you want more information, you'll have to buy the book The Doctor's Book of Food Remedies. I subscribe to so many letters. They give me some of the remedies to entice me and then they try to sell the books. Maybe you can talk the libraries into buying them.

To continue about the nuts, if you snack on nuts four times a week, you cut the risk of fatal heart attacks almost in half. Another food that has power to reduce heart attacks are mushrooms.

I'm practicing a lot of this information and then I think, "What am I doing?" On one hand I say I've lived long enough and have peace in my heart and am ready to go, and then I'm doing all these good things that will make me live longer. Then I rationalize and say "Well, I'll live better for as long as it lasts."

Now I have some partial good news for you. If you want all the good news you have to buy the doctor's book, but here's what they gave me. All fibers help block absorption of calories and fat, so you'll be improving the outside of your body as well as the inside of your body. I like that.

Here's a bit of humor - why are so fish so thin? Because they eat fish. So much for fish stories.

Now I'll give you some good news about fish. Fish give lots of lean, high protein as well as healthful omega-3 fats that help clean out arteries. That's why Eskimos have very few heart attacks and are slim. These acids in fish also reduce pain and inflammation of arthritis, lower your risk of cancer, and help to prevent dementia and depression. Make sure your fish are not high in mercury: I hope I saved you some money.

The Soup of Life

Recently, my son Dan has been trying to get me to persuade the Valone family and the Leone family to make tapes whenever possible or write down things about our families before they are lost in memory. The other day there was an article in the Observer that said the same thing. I think the Valones will be OK. I have a great niece who tackles that sort of thing. As for the Leones, there's no interest unless I start writing stories I remember. I'll just tell you about the experience my father had in WW I in Italy.

I had never heard that the Army doctors ran out of anesthetic and were operating without it. My father was all shot up - arms, legs and chest. The surgeons wanted to amputate some of his limbs, but he refused. So they operated as best they could without anesthetics. He had one arm shorter than the other and one leg shorter, plus when he died at 75, he still had shrapnel in his chest. When he came home, he was an invalid for two years. My mother had to dress him and feed him. Then one day he got mad and willed himself to be well. It worked and it worked for me when I had heart problems. His advice to me was, "Just remember you're ¾ spiritual and ¼ physical. The body is nothing. The mind is everything". Maybe it can help someone out there like it did me. I always felt healthy.

Does this bore you or can you share some of your stories with us? Let me know.

Margaret Valone

Come On, Get Healthy

I think spring is a good time to inspect our bodies and our health because one of the prime reasons for obesity is lack of exercise. The warm weather will encourage you to get out and walk or bicycle. Later on you can swim. Your mind will get more active as summer goes on.

We are going to take a test - true or false:
1. Green tea is good for your heart.
2. Coffee is a diuretic that dehydrates you.
3. All meats are linked to colon cancer.
4. Apple cider vinegar cures arthritis.
5. Carb rich foods are fattening.
6. Vitamin B fights cancer.
7. Aspartame sweetener is dangerous.
8. Spray cooking oils turn into trans fats.
9. You need 8 glasses of water a day.
10. Saw palmetto wards off prostate cancer.

All these statements are false!

A recent major study of 120,000 men says it's OK to take that second cup of coffee. It will not be a risk to your heart! Now they have found eggs provide a number of heart healthy nutrients such as folate, vitamin E and B-12, plus omega-3 and omega-6 fatty acids.

It was discovered that Internet hucksters were selling apple-cider vinegar as a cure for arthritis, high cholesterol, and osteoporosis, all false. But here's something to be warned about. Vinegar tablets can damage your esophagus.

The Soup of Life

Don't be afraid to cook with Pam. It's OK.

Four 8-ounce glasses of water a day is sufficient especially if you have a heart problem and you retain water.

Good news! Dark chocolate can lower your blood pressure.

A lot of chicken may reduce the risk of colon cancer.

More good news: carrots are good for your eyes. They contain zinc antioxidants to ward off macular degeneration.

Sweet potatoes and spinach are also healthy choices

Although green tea has no help for the heart, it does reduce the risk of ovarian cancer in women.

Don't worry about mercury in fish - but avoid the smoked variety because they lose omega-3 fatty acids and are high in sodium.

Here's some really good news! Starchy foods like bread, rice, pasta and cereals are low in fat and calories. It's the butter, sour cream, or mayonnaise that do the damage. Take less of those.

Men will really celebrate this news. A 1,000 unit of vitamin D daily might reduce the risk of colon and prostate cancer. For the women it helps ovarian and breast cancer.

People who have used Echinacea to fight colds are wasting their money. Chicken soup and tissues can replace this flower extract.

All this information comes from Freidman School of Nutrition Science, a world-renowned research center.

How many of you like to stretch a lot? As a kid growing up, I stretched a lot every night when I went to bed. I often wondered if that was why I was the tallest of the girls in our family. Now I read from the experts regular stretching can I improve your flexibility, reduce stiffness, improve circulation, promote better posture, stress relief, and relaxation. It also enhances your coordination and balance and reduces your risk of injury. Boy, am I going to go back to stretching I'm trying to get in shape for my trip in October.

I hope I have motivated you with all this information to improve your health! They are making us live longer so I guess we're going to have to shape up on our own! I wish I knew who "they" are!

Now it's time to finish up with a laugh at my expense. This is a humility story that I couldn't stop laughing at! I was wearing more than a bathing suit, so I think it's OK. We need hearty laughs. This morning I was putting on a sleeveless blouse. I checked to see if it was even. I hate when I button up a shirt and I get down to the bottom and find out it's lopsided, so I thought, I'll button the bottom button first to avoid a problem. Well, I had my breakfast, got all my recycling stuff together and went out back to get them ready for the trash pick-up. On the way back I saw a young man working on his car next door. I asked him if he lived over Time Pieces. He said no, but his friend did. I asked him to let me know if he's going to put things out for Attic and Seller Days because I don't want to be alone. He agreed so I continued into the house. I happened to look down and my blouse was all open! I forgot to button all the other buttons! Isn't old age fun? Oh, well, it could have been worse. I could have been wearing a bikini! It's fun to laugh at yourself!

The Soup of Life

Weight and Health

I have good news for you. You are going to have a healthier year this year. How do I know? I know because I have subscribed to the Mayo Clinic Health Letter and their supplement called *Special Report*. It's full of health hints and they are a reputable medical center, so they know what they are talking about.

I'll give the information in doses, just like medicine. I also have information from the *Harvard Women's Health Watch*. Gee, it looks like I'm going to have to do a lot of homework, but you're worth it. I like to share the wealth and this is going to be a wealth of knowledge which hopefully will help you keep more of your wealth.

There's only one thing that bothers me. There's too much talk about learning how to be 100 years old or more. I want to feel good but not to live so long. There are so many things I used to do that I can't do now. How many more things will there be that I can't do if I live to be 100? But hopefully I can help our lives be healthier for a while. Here goes.

One of the first health areas they addressed was obesity. Even if you reduce your body fat 5-10 percent, you will lose weight. Now take special note of this fact: lasting success in losing weight involves a long-term commitment to building healthy habits that last a lifetime. We have to make healthy eating habits and have a regular exercise program and stick to it. If we will do these things, we will be more confident, more energetic, stronger and more self sufficient.

I have included a chart that gives a healthy weight for your height (see below). Please keep this chart for your guide.

Even if you don't make your goal, getting closer to the goal is progress. Keep in mind the amount of fat you are carrying and where it's located make a big difference.

This is a start. I'll insert information to help you. I'll try not to make it like a crash course in college. The letter promises "delicious meals, convenience in the kitchen, optimum nutrition and allows you to eat your favorite food." We'll see.

	Normal		Overweight					Obese			
BMI	19	24	25	26	27	28	29	30	35	40	45	50
Height	Weight In Pounds										
4'10"	91	115	119	124	129	134	138	143	167	191	215	239
4'11"	94	119	124	128	133	138	143	148	173	198	222	247
5'0"	97	123	128	133	138	143	148	153	179	204	230	255
5'1"	100	127	132	137	143	148	153	158	185	211	238	264
5'2"	104	131	136	142	147	153	158	164	191	218	246	273
5'3"	107	135	141	146	152	158	163	169	197	225	254	282
5'4"	110	140	145	151	157	163	169	174	204	232	262	291
5'5"	114	144	150	156	162	168	174	180	210	240	270	300
5'6"	118	148	155	161	167	173	179	186	216	247	278	309
5'7"	121	153	159	166	172	178	185	191	223	255	287	319
5'8"	125	158	164	171	177	184	190	197	230	262	295	328
5'9"	128	162	169	176	182	189	195	203	236	270	304	338
5'10"	132	167	174	181	188	195	202	209	243	278	313	348
5'11"	136	172	179	186	193	200	208	215	250	286	322	358
6'0"	140	177	184	191	199	205	213	221	258	294	331	368
6'1"	144	182	189	197	204	212	219	227	265	302	340	378
6'2"	148	186	194	202	210	218	225	233	272	311	350	389
6'3"	152	192	200	208	216	224	232	240	279	319	359	399
6'4"	156	197	205	213	221	230	238	246	287	328	369	410

The Soup of Life

Diving into Healthy Habits

People often ask me, where do you find all that material you write about? Well, I keep having new experiences. For example, my cousin, Carolyn Patton, talked me into getting a membership to use the pool at the Ramada Inn. I was looking for some exercise I could do and that sounded good. It was just what the doctor ordered. Actually, we met many people there who were using the pool for therapy after bone surgeries. As for me, my blood pressure has come down and I feel like a million after an hour in the pool. The other day, I used the bicycle and Carolyn used the treadmill. At first my legs were tight, but that wore off and it was great.

The bonus is the wonderful people we meet. Some are workers, some are swimmers. We have made many new friends. I love to see families in the pool, especially fathers with the children. You learn a lot about people in a pool. You can predict the children that will be well adjusted and those that will have problems because they never go far enough to please their parents and love is withheld. How sad.

One day, there were three generations in the pool. The grandmother was treating her two sons and their families. This was grandma's treat because they all had worked on a project together. She was teaching them that work is rewarding and appreciated. It was a pleasure watching this family - they encouraged the children, but never criticized their efforts. Also, they were all so polite. I saw all of this and loved it. You never know what people you see.

We met a family from England. They have a son working in

Toronto and they were holidaying at the Ramada. It was fun.

I've been amazed at the small children, actually babies, that are in the water. One little boy I called the "personality kid", would jump into his mother's arms, go underwater, and come up laughing.

Then there is the hot tub that people enjoy. We can't go in because of our heart conditions but I would love it. You can feel like you're at a spa and it's all right under our noses.

Well, I've bicycled this year, but I haven't shot my baskets yet. I must do that before snow flies. If I don't, that will be one more thing I don't do anymore. I want to thank you for the response to my Bible class. We are meeting every Thursday at 10 a.m. at my house.

There's room for more. I can seat 20 at tables and more on the couches. I don't play poker, but a full house sounds good to me. It's no more work for me except trying to remember names. I prepare lesson plans and then it doesn't matter if there are 2, 20, or 200. Even if you're just curious, come and join us. All you need is an open mind and a heart to match.

Here's a thought for the day; the best exercise to strengthen your heart is to stoop down and pick up someone who needs your help - either physically, spiritually, emotionally, or financially.

Isn't that great? Look for people who need you, follow through and receive the reward of joy.

Healthful Hints

Today's column will contain information on getting healthy and staying healthy. All this information is good for your health only if you use it. Weigh yourself every day at the same time on the same scale, wearing little or no clothes. I even blow my nose, brush my teeth and take a shower first. Every little bit helps. Keep track on a calendar.

Avoid alcohol and too much liquid. Juices, tea, and coffee all add up. Ask your doctor how much your total should be and stick to it. Watch for swelling in ankles, legs, and belly. If they occur, call your doctor.

The following is information for people with heart problems. If you are breathing easily, your weight is on target and you have little or no swelling, you take your medicine, weigh yourself, watch your diet and exercise, then go out and enjoy yourself or do some of those chores you're neglected.

Now here are the things you look out for that spell trouble:
1. If you're having trouble breathing with activity or at night.
2. If you gain 2 pounds in one day or 3 to 5 pounds in a week.
3. If your chest feels heavy or tight, but gets better with rest, you feel tired and you have a constant cough, call your doctor. Maybe you need to change your medicine.

Now here are the signs that should send you for medical help.
1. Hard to breathe, even when resting.
2. Chest pains or chest feels heavy or tight.
3. You're sweating and feel weak or faint. Don't waste time. If you can't get your doctor, go to the hospital.

Margaret Valone

I'm happy to say most people with heart problems work and enjoy life. I'm one of them but if the symptoms I described take place, go into action fast.

Now I'm going to tell you how to be healthy by watching your sodium intake. First of all, learn to read the labels on food before you buy. When dining out, go for vegetables like lettuce greens, fresh mushrooms, fresh fruits, and hard-boiled eggs. Limit use of steak sauce and ketchup. Go light on heavy sauces, gravy and creamy salad dressing - ask for these things on the side. Avoid croutons, olives, shredded cheese and pickles.

On the other hand, avoid these words: basted, au gratin, braised, buttered, cheese, cream, or butter sauce, creamed, crispy, scalloped, fried, hash, Hollandaise, pan roasted, pot pie, rich, sautéed or stewed with bacon or sausage.

We're all fearful of doctor bills and hospital bills. Well, all this information can help you from having either. Be smart. Use this information for your good health and pocket book.

Now I'm going to hit a little bit about a serious and costly problem of obesity. We have it in children, adults, both male and female. Am I right? What can we do about it? Let's be honest - the foods that are best for us are costly. Last Saturday I went to the farmer's market. One pepper cost $1. Unbelievable. Well, I did find a farmer who gave me two large peppers for $1. I suggest that if it's possible for you and your children, go pick your own. If I can find some blackberries, I'm going to pick my own. One day I picked over 100 quarts. It wasn't a crime for 12-year-olds to work at that time. I'll have to check out Walker's cherry trees. I don't think I'll climb, but maybe some branches are low enough.

This year I'm going to encourage people to have their own gardens either at home or someplace else. I have two tomato plants in two buckets. Last year I did well. I don't have a green thumb - only a blue finger.

I'm going to give you some generalities that have helped me.

For breakfast I have fruit and Quaker Oats.

The Soup of Life

For lunch I have half a sandwich and an apple for or a small dish of leftover spaghetti, lentil soup, or chicken soup with short macaroni.

For supper I'll have a pork chop, some baked beans and potatoes sliced and done in the microwave for eight minutes.

For dessert I have chocolate pudding or cookies dipped in milk.

Here are two absolute musts:
1. Don't eat between meals.
2. Take smaller portions. I also limit my bread to two slices per day. Sometimes more.

Try to eliminate desserts.

Now there's something we have to address for the children. They are probably watching too much TV and eating while they are watching. Parents, you have to be parents and control this duo of habits.

Check each other out every day and supper. Don't yell, but encourage your children if they are not in the program and be sure to praise them if they are trying.

And kids, check your parents the same way. Get together with your friends or families and get on this program. We can't afford to get sick or buy new clothes, right?

Margaret Valone

How to Be Happy and Healthy

I have some good news for veterans. I had a call recently from the Jamestown VA outpatient clinic. It is a new clinic that has lab services, primary care, social workers, psychiatrists, X-ray department, colonoscopies and benefit officers for non-medical needs. If you want information, call 716-338-1511. It's so good to know all about these services and to have them so close.

Here are some truisms I like:

Fear is the opposite of faith, and fear tolerated is faith contaminated. I think this is very needful for these distressing times. Don't tolerate fear. It will get you down. Think positive and know your fearful conditions are temporary. Whatever you do, don't be alone. Call friends in or go out with friends. If there are activities going on in schools or churches, attend them. Go for walks, too. That's so therapeutic!

I found another thought I had written down. Don't think of what others have. Think of what you have to give away. We usually think of their money, beautiful cars and houses, good paying jobs or elevated titles, lots of degrees, etc. But if you really want to feel good, think of all the problems they have. They may not be healthy or good-looking or have people skills or be very friendly. Where is the love? That's where you can be richer than all of them! Wish them love.

Let's talk about health. We need good health to make us more productive and save money from not needing doctors. How do we prevent catching the common cold? Be sure to keep your head and feet dry and warm. Survivors know this is true because that saved

The Soup of Life

them. Dress for the season indoors and out. Use the layered look so that you can add clothing or remove it.

Eat properly. Don't overeat but eat a balanced diet. For breakfast I usually have a handful of peanuts, three prunes, four tablespoons of cooked oats and an apple. I have no idea where I got these amounts but they work for me. It keeps my weight down. For lunch, try a sandwich or a half plus vegetables. The more colored they are the more nutritious they are. I like to munch on small carrots. For supper, I usually have meat or fish, a potato, and regular salad. You can put a roast in the crock-pot, I usually put it on high for one hour and then on low for three hours. I like to do this on Sunday mornings. Then when I get back from church, the meat is perfect. I usually cook fish with seasoned bread crumbs, of course, they are Italian style, and fry them in oil at medium to low flame until they brown. So good! As for my potato, I can bake it or slice it thin with the skin on and season the slices with pepper (black), medium hot pepper flakes, Mrs. Dash table and original blends. You can make your own seasoning if you can eat salt. I mix them up, put them in a covered microwave bowl for five minutes. Then I add my ketchup as I'm eating. This is my own idea. I enjoy it. Maybe I already told you. Remember the old song Blame it on My Youth? Well, blame it on my old age!

We must also make a schedule of exercising. This should depend on your health and age. Walking is good for everyone, bicycling and swimming are beneficial, too. These physical activities also help your mental state of health. The secret to good mental health is to look for relationships. Deepen those you already have and start new ones. If you concentrate and feed on yourself, you'll starve. Mingle with people that laugh a lot. That's one good trait that is contagious. It's like medicine. Don't hang around a lot of pills. They are contagious too and will bring you down. Read a lot and think a lot. It's good for your mental health.

I forgot to tell you how to treat a runny nose. I was told to heat up some tomato soup. Add butter and lots of black pepper. Put on a pair of sweat pants and go to bed. Sweat it out.

I found some cures. Activated charcoal pills will take poisons out of your system. (I don't know what that means). Use vinegar and honey for allergies. Roll lemon on your head to get rid of a headache. A cleaning tip: always clean your house from top to bottom. That will allow the dust to settle before you vacuum.

Life's Little Remedies

Get your paper and pen ready. I'm going to give you information on how to feed good health and treat what ails you. Got this information from *Prevention Magazine*, the June issue.

1. If you're stressed out, grab a banana. It only has 105 calories and 14 grams of sugar. It fills you up, boosts your sugar and gives you 30 percent of daily vitamin B6, which helps the brain to produce serotonin. It should bring peace. This is great news except if you have to keep away from potassium (like I do), you can't eat bananas.
2. A handful of raisins, 60 raisins, contain 1 gram of fiber and 212 mg. of potassium. Wines and juices are effective in maintaining cardiovascular health and bring down blood sugar. So far I'm not helping my brain or my heart.
3. Here's a good way to take care of gassy and constipated feelings. Take 1½ cups of live cultured yogurt. This pushes food easier through the gastrointestinal tract. Yogurt also helps to digest beans and dairy lactose, which can cause gas.
4. Want to prevent kidney stones? Eat eight dried apricot halves. They have 2 grams of fiber, 3 mg. of sodium, and 325 mg. of potassium. These will help keep minerals from accumulating in urine and forming calcium oxalate stones, the most common type of kidney stones.
5. Feeling low and anxious? Take 3 ounces of canned white tuna (800 mg. of omega-3s). If you want to be seafood-free, munch on a small bagel. This contains 37 grams of carbs which will give you a dose of mood-boosting serotonin.
6. Ginger tea will help against nausea caused by motion sickness or pregnancy without causing dry mouth or drowsiness.

7. Guess what helps gut pain, diarrhea, cramping or nausea? Pile on a lot of basil in your cooking or in your salads.
8. Here's a money saver to calm a cough: take 2 teaspoons of thick, dark, brown honey. This is great for children who have a cough. Honey contains antioxidants and antimicrobial properties.
9. If you are prone to ulcers, try a cup of cut up cabbage.
10. A 3-ounce serving of turkey will help you sleep better.
11. The fiber in 4 dried figs helps a hemorrhoid problem by providing 5 percent potassium and 10 percent manganese.
12. If you have a yeast infection, load up on garlic which can inhibit the growth of the candida albicans fungus, which is the culprit in the pain, itch and vaginal discharge of yeast infections. Include garlic in sauces, salad dressings, and marinades.
13. Chamomile tea helps heartburn, digestive inflammation, spasms, and gas. Put 2 teaspoons in 10 ounces of water (very hot) for 20 minutes covering the cup to keep essential oils in water. You may have to drink the tea a few times a day for complete relief.

Now let's laugh a little.

When we were young, the two-step was a dance. When you get old, it's the way you come down the stairs. (My original).

There was this little boy who was getting dressed to go to school. His mother wanted to put a V-neck sweater over his shirt. "Oh, no," he cried. "Every time my teacher wears a V-neck and bends over, her lungs fall out."

I have another cute story about a very young student who adored his teacher. One day, one of the boys said, "She's nice, but she's fat." The other boy quickly went to her defense. "Only when she bends over." There we see both sides of the spectrum. One is critical and the other is loving. We always seem to forget, we do have a choice.

The Soup of Life

Live Healthier and Happier

Today's column is going to be filled with information that could save your life. It comes from a publication called *Nutrition Action Healthletter*. Here is some of the information you can consider:

Did you know Marie Callender's chicken pot pie is among the unhealthiest frozen entrees and that Campbell's condensed soups are among the unhealthiest soups you can eat?

With information like this, it's no wonder the publication has readers approaching two million and is the world's largest circulation health newsletter. It is independent and contains no advertising. They have the freedom to blow whistles on products that have false advertising and recommend the good ones.

If you want to avoid diet-related diseases like heart attacks, stroke, cancer, diabetes, and osteoporosis, the information contained in this publication can prolong your life and sometimes cure your ills.

Good news. Supplements like calcium, vitamin D, and folic acid offer real health benefits, but here are some claims that have not been proven: Ginsana for energy loss or stress; Promensil red clover extract for hot flashes; and Garlique garlic for lowering cholesterol. And beware of this, some supplements like selenium, beta carotene and St. John's Wort might even harm you. Be safe. Let this publication guide you.

How many times have you asked yourself which is better for you - butter or margarine? Scientific research says tub and spray margarine are better than butter. Also avoid stick margarine because it is loaded with partially hydrogenated vegetable oil. The fats in this oil raises your bad cholesterol and promotes heart disease.

Can you have sweets and still lose weight? Sugar-free foods like cake, cookies, ice cream and candies may be loaded with calories. Read the labels. Acesulfame potassium, Nutrasweet, and saccharin may promote cancer, and sugar alcohols like sorbitol may cause diarrhea. On the bright side, Splenda and rebiana (stevia) appear to be safe.

Now I eat a lot of fruit and here's what I found out. Watermelon, grapefruit, kiwi and cantaloupe are the best. All the fruits that I eat like cherries, strawberries, apples, and peaches are likely to be contaminated with dangerous contaminates. I'll scrub them more thoroughly. I like them too much! Sure, now they tell me. Where were they when I was young?

Did you know a dish of spaghetti and meatballs at Olive Garden has the calories and saturated fat of two McDonald's Big Macs?

The editors of this publication said you can live healthier, happier, save time, live longer and eat tastier foods. I think they have a lot to offer you. I'll give you the address and you can check it out and decide for yourself. It's only $24 a year. It is: Nutrition Action Healthletter, an independent newsletter on nutrition, diet and food safety published for consumers by the nonprofit Center for Science in the Public Interest; 1220 L St., N.W. Suite 300 Washington, D.C. 20005

For more information on Nutrition Action, visit: www.cspinet.org/nah/index.htm.

Now I'll finish with some humor which I know is good for your health. I'm not on commission; I only care about your life. I try to make it happier but I'm not a doctor.

OK, now let's laugh. This is a story about a painter. He came up with an idea. He told his men if they put paint thinner in their paint, it would go on easier and they'd use less time and less paint.

The Soup of Life

So they did. That night the painter couldn't sleep. He knew that he was being dishonest. Well, he finally fell asleep. In his dream, he heard a deep voice saying, "Repaint you thinner."

Now tell me, did you laugh or did you groan? You can't win them all.

Here's a good thought for the day: life is measured by your donations, not but your duration.

Margaret Valone

Dreams, Dollars and Diets

I dream a lot. Some of it is in my head and some of it is in my bed.

In my head, I dream about beautiful places and people, about nature and love. In my bed, I dream about all kinds of things. I'm going to tell you about my dream last night and I want you to analyze it.

I dreamed a woman who was a stranger to me gave me a ride in a red pickup truck. The roof over her head was metal, but on my side I was covered by a tarp and it had a hole in it.

Alongside the road there was a zoo. She wanted to see what kind of reaction she would get from the lions if she tooted her horn.

Well, when that lion heard the horn, he jumped over the fence, made a beeline for me and the hole in the tarp. I screamed and fell out of bed. It's a good thing I'm dense - no, not my head, but my bones. I wasn't hurt.

Now a friend of mine said the color red, the lion and the tarp with a hole in it stood for different things. I won't tell you what she said because I want you to have a clear head and tell me what you see. Isn't life exciting?

The Soup of Life

Did you notice when you shopped last time how the prices have gone up? Holy cow! The only thing I see going down around here is the temperature! And that will make our gas bills higher!

Speaking about expenses, last week I had a new guest at my Sunday dinner. He brought an ice cream cake. It was delicious. Would you believe the company that put it out was "Mudd"? Is that good business? I'd change my name or use someone else's. But I must admit, it was fantastic. Guess what it cost? $17! That's not dirt cheap! In light of all these expenses, I thought I'd give you a few hints on how to save money.

1. Clean glass with ¼ cup vinegar in a pint-size bottle filled with water.
2. Clean your floors with ½ cup vinegar and a gallon of water. Mop and dry.
3. You can make an all-purpose cleaner by using a teaspoon of Borax and a quart of warm water. If you want to cut grease, add a splash of lemon juice or white vinegar.
4. You can deodorize your carpets by sprinkling baking soda, wait 15 minutes, then vacuum.
5. Instead of aerosol air fresheners, put some cinnamon and cloves in a pot of boiling water.
6. To make a disinfectant, use ¼ cup of Borax in ½ gallon of hot water.
7. Did you know that regular ketchup will make copper bottoms shine? It works great!

There don't you love to save money? I hate it when I spend a whole bunch of money and there's nothing to eat!

Which reminds me, last week I started my diet of Quaker Oats twice a day. I take raisins, prunes, apples and nuts with it and then at night I have a regular meal. I lost two pounds. If I could lose two pounds every week, maybe I'll fit better in the coffin! Just joking. It's strange the things that I laugh at these days.

Keep laughing. It's great for your health and you'll have wrinkles in the right places.

Health Help

I'm going to give you some health advice taken from the Mayo Clinic health letter. We're going to start by discussing chronic pain. There are several types of pain such as back pain, headaches, or facial pain. The pain could even be wide-spread such as fibromyalgia.

When medication or medical treatments do not work it can start a downward spiral of frustration, decreased functioning, stress, isolation, or discouragement.

However, there is help and hope through numerous pain rehabilitation centers across the country. They usually cannot make your pain go away, but individualized care from a team of specialists can help you change your focus to live a more fulfilling life. I would have just said, "The less you do, the less you want to do. Get going!" But what I think doesn't count because I do not charge.

When my sister Louise was having a bout with depression, I would tell her words of encouragement, but all she would say was, "I know. You don't tell me anything my doctor doesn't say, but unless I pay for it, it doesn't count." How about that?

To continue with the Mayo Clinic letter, it says we seek help with:
1. Physical therapy. It gives you better posture, proper body mechanics and pain related behaviors.
2. Stress management; how to relax, meditate, and plan your day
3. Psychological care; lifestyle management, group therapy

The Soup of Life

and family counseling. They might even use acupuncture and hypnosis.

Now let's say you do not have the money to take all these courses of action, so we'll try to use common sense and break it down. You know what kind of pain you have so I do not have to try to figure it out. They start with home measures that don't work and you get worse; thanks a lot.

Next, they say little about physical therapy. I say walk a lot. At first, walk slowly and do not go too far. The next day, you walk faster and further. If you can ride a bike, do the same thing. If you have access to a pool, do the same method as well. Stretch a lot throughout the day and concentrate on your posture.

As for stress management, they say learn to relax. You can try meditation and prayer. Get dressed so that you feel you look good. Walk to the library and get a good book that will make you laugh and read it. Tomorrow, go dress shopping. The next day, go grocery shopping. The next day, go browsing. If you have to go alone, so be it. Chances are you have friends or family to go with you. I also find it good to be around young people and children.

Lastly, they say rehabilitation centers may give you psychological care. I think the things we mentioned above could classify in that department. I cannot help you with acupuncture or hypnosis, but I do have a couple friends who rub my back and crack my back.

I hope these suggestions help. No, you do not have to pay me - I'm good for nothing.

They found out that drugs, angiogenesis receptor blockers, used to reduce high blood pressure, also helps dementia. Ask your doctor.

Margaret Valone

Hints on Gout

Today, I have more health information that will prove profitable. I'm going to give you information which is good for a healthy colon. The principle in general is to eat a high fiber diet and I'll tell you how. There are two types of fiber: insoluble and soluble. They both aid digestion and get this, they both help maintain a healthy weight! Insoluble- fiber is found in whole grains, cereals, certain fruits and vegetables, such as apple skin, corn and carrots. These insoluble fiber foods can help prevent constipation and helps reduce the risk of certain types of cancer. Soluble fibers are found in oats, beans and certain fruits and vegetables such as strawberries and peas.

Soluble fiber can reduce cholesterol which may help lower the risk of heart disease and helps control blood sugar levels.

The following foods are high in fiber:
1. Eat six to eight ounces a day of wheat and bran cereals, whole-wheat muffins or toast, and corn tortillas with your meals.
2. Try to eat two cups of fruit per day. Apples, oranges, strawberries, and bananas are all good. Fruit juices are low in fiber.
3. Try to eat three cups of vegetables a day. Carrots, asparagus, broccoli, peas, and corn are good.
4. One cup of beans a day is healthful. Try navy beans and chickpeas. One cup of cooked lentils has 15 grams of fiber.
5. A small handful of seeds like sunflower seeds is good for you.

The Soup of Life

If you are on a 2,000 calorie diet, you should aim for 31 grams of fiber per day and get used to reading food labels. Maybe you can share this information with a family member or friend.

The cause of gout is high blood level of uric acid, a waste product. The waste product is a breakdown of purines which are substances naturally found in the body. Purines are also found in foods such as liver, brain, kidney, sweet bread, anchovies, mackerel, mince meat, scallops and herring. Chicken, meat and fish have lesser amounts of purines so they can be eaten in moderation. Avoid drinking alcohol all together or drink moderately. Here's a suggested menu:
1. Breakfast - cereals and breads, coffee, tea, oatmeal, eggs, fruits, juices, low-fat cheese, milk, peanut butter.
2. Lunch - nuts and peanut butter, pasta, soups cream style, low-fat cheeses and broth.
3. Dinner - pasta, macaroni, eggs, vegetables, breads and cereals, low-fat cheeses and soups.

Other foods low in purines are gelatin, fats and oils in small amounts, soda, sugar, syrups and other sweets in moderation. The key to a low purine diet is moderation.

Here are more foods with moderate purine levels: beef, lamb, pork, vegetables such it as mushrooms, asparagus, cauliflower, spinach, wheat germ, all types of yeast, and gravies.

All this information came from Lisa McDowell's book "Cure Gout Now." There's a lot of good information in this column. I suggest you cut it out and save it. A friend of mine did this research for me and I'm just passing it on. That's what we do - we help whenever and whomever we can. If we eat better, we'll feel better!

Now I'm going to give you some tips about dealing with gout or arthritis. New research has found evidence that compounds in cherries may help relieve pain. A couple, who are friends, brought me a bottle of concentrated cherry juice ($15). Wasn't that sweet of them? I must confess it helped a lot!

How does it work? For one, cherries lower levels of uric acid in the blood. Uric acid is one of the most common causes of gout pain. A study done by the University of California showed that taking a serving of cherries daily significantly lowered the blood uric acid in women by as much as 15 percent. Dried cherries or cherry juice also make an impact.

The element that makes cherries so beneficial is called "anthocyanins". Taking cherries on a regular basis helps relieve inflammation and also reduces the risk of colon cancer. Also, you can choose either sweet or sour cherries; they both have the same benefits. Normal amounts that are recommended every day are two tablespoons of tart cherry juice concentrate or one to two servings of fresh or dried cherries. Not everyone reacts the same. Some people use the cherries with a low purine diet. Cherry juice for gout relief has been used around the world for hundreds of years, but only recently the mainstream media has brought it to light.

While some people are skeptical about the benefits of cherry juice in the treatment of gout and arthritis, many more are finding that it is a wonderful way to take control of their pain and get moving again with the help of a very easy and delicious cure.

The Soup of Life

Choices and Good Health

In the last couple of columns we have talked about the tangible things (those we can touch and feel) and the physical things in our lives we can touch and feel, but we can't change about ourselves and others. Then we talked about the abstract things in our lives that we have the power to change. There are the things of the mind, the heart and soul. What does it take to change your mind? You don't even have to move. The fact that you have changed your mind isn't even visible. But the action that takes place from you changing your mind is visible.

I thought about making up a mind game. We could call it "Choice".

Do you choose to laugh or cry?

Do you choose to smile or frown?

Do you choose to get involved or sit back?

Use different choices with different results. We could make a game of it or write different stories.

Will you send me some choices you and your family came up with? I'll make you up a story from your choices. You can write a story of your own. We can see how we can influence lives - the lives of others as well as our own. I'm game (pardon the pun) if you are. Let's have some fun.

I'm going to tell you a story. Then I'll leave it open-ended and you can pick it up and add your choices. You can carry it to the end or you can write a few paragraphs and leave it open-ended for someone else to pick up. Or if you have a good ending, end it, and we'll start another story. Maybe we can form a writer's club. This would be great fun for people with creative minds.

Last Friday my doctor pricked my gout finger until white liquid-like milk came out of it. Then she asked me questions. Do I eat nuts? Yes, a lot of nuts for protein. No, no, no. Any kind of nuts are forbidden with gout. Then she asked me if I ate chocolate. I said until recently, I used it modestly, but my niece from California came with the good news that dark chocolate is good for your heart, so we had dark chocolate coming out our ears. Then the doctor said "No, no, no. This is bad for gout."

I had to give up my slice of bread with peanut butter to provide my protein as part of my breakfast. I'll have to go back to cereal.

Then I had more good news. One of my health periodicals gave a report about a study they did for four years. They divided the people into two groups.

One group got placebos and the other medication. At the end of the four years the ones that were taking medication were slightly better, but they forgot to make a record of the degree of the problem each person had in each group. So they really couldn't come to any conclusions. Can you believe that? And I paid good money for their expertise.

You know what I am thinking? I was brought up on home remedies. Maybe they just kept me going until I could pay a doctor. I'll never know.

Here's a list of foods gout patients should put in their diets:
1. One clove of garlic a day.
2. One and a half cups of kidney or any other beans daily.
3. Non-fat milk, up to five glasses a day. Each glass is 30 mg of calcium.
4. Eat one or two oranges (heavy skin and deep color) daily.
5. Salmon (fish oil) one serving per week, three ounces baked.
6. Tofu, half a cup daily.
7. Tomato sauce or a few sauces a week (without cheese).
8. Juices, coffee, soups, milk (cool water is better than hot)

The Soup of Life

Now I'll tell you which of these items I can't use. I'm supposed to drink eight ounces of water, four times a day (so I won't retain water. There goes the non-fat milk.

I can't eat orange or citrus fruit because I'm on Coumadin. Tofu is also out for me.

So what are we saying? What you make on the bananas you lose on the oranges, -but you know what I mean. You gain some, you lose some. It looks like I'm going to have gout in my finger for a long time.

Now some of this information will help some people. Check it out. I could say take it with a grain of salt, but I can't use salt.

I wish you could see me. I'm laughing my head off. Life is great if you don't lose your sense of humor. I hope you laughed.

By the way, the medical report I gave was research on non-steroidal anti-inflammatory drugs once thought to help prevent Alzheimer's disease. The periodical is called *Mind, Mood and Memory* sent through Massachusetts General Hospital. Just so you know I didn't make it up.

Margaret Valone

Cooking up Some Fun

A couple of weeks ago I was a guest of Brooks Memorial Hospital at a luncheon at the Shorewood Country Club. Everything was very nice. It's kind of them to show the volunteers how much they are appreciated. I had a bonus from this meal.

It was delicious. The meat was strips of beef rolled with a tasty filling. I couldn't eat it all so I brought some home. Now what was I going to do with these leftovers? I came up with an idea. I cut the strips in small pieces. I opened up a can of College Inn Beef Broth and put it in a frying pan. Then I added diced carrot sticks, two small red potatoes-diced, pieces of celery and celery leaves and cut up half an onion. Then I seasoned with garlic powder, black pepper and a little crushed red pepper. Keeping a low flame, I covered the top and let it cook. It could be a beef stew or later I could separate some broth and add some of my cooked elbow macaroni which I keep on hand, I got three meals for myself out of that.

While I was in a cooking mood, I made a couple of chicken dishes, Instead of using beef broth, I substituted Fit & Active Chicken Broth, then used the same ingredients plus a chicken leg and a thigh. I cooked the whole thing until the chicken was tender. While I was still in the mood, I cut up three more legs and thighs and put them in the crock-pot with some diluted cream of chicken soup. I usually cook the meats on high for one hour and then put the setting at low. Usually I'll let everything cook for three hours although I'm sure they could be eaten much sooner. Season to taste. I felt good about myself because I had several meals ready to be served. Everything was so delicious I didn't even need Romano cheese. I find that we are creatures of habit. If we always put

The Soup of Life

cheese on all macaronis then we continue to do so even when it tastes good without. Actually that's waste. Use it on something else.

And who says you have to have dessert with every meal? And does it have to be pastry? Can fruit be okay? It certainly helps to keep the weight down. By the way, I don't get paid for this but I find Tuscany's Pecorino Romano cheese very good and very reasonable. Maybe the competition will bring some other cheese prices down. If I get other tips I'll pass them on.

By the way, I had a great time at the senior prom! As I left the house, college kids were all over my porch and the grass. "Where are you going", they asked. No, I wasn't wearing a gown but I was dressed up more than usual. I told them I was going to the senior prom. We all laughed. The high school kids always put on a good night's entertainment. Unfortunately there were fewer people than last year. I guess the swine flu scared people away. There were only four men there. The women last longer. How come the women wait on the men and they still outlive them? What can we learn from that? Does putting others first give you a longer life? Does work improve your health? I wouldn't be surprised.

Next time you want something done, ask your husband to do it so he'll live longer. Think it will work?

Margaret Valone

POLITICAL

Thinking Deeply about Government Issues

Sometimes people who are close to me ask the question, "Why do you always have to go overboard?" Maybe that's because I want to get in deep water. It's easier to swim in deeper water than shallow water and I like a challenge. I guess this is the way I feel about people. I have no time for shallow people. I like deep thinkers who accept challenges.

When I was a teenager, I remember that while other kids and friends were jumping off the breakwall, I was diving in. I felt more in control by putting my hands up to come up. Some people don't want to get wet and some people want the security of standing up in the water. Each of us has his comfort zone, but can't comfort zones change as we get older? When we become more mature, isn't it OK to care about other people's needs as well as our own?

Going back to the original question, these people were talking about going overboard on issues. I care deeply about unfairness, injustice; the needy need our help and the greedy must be stopped. Sometimes I am upset over actions that have been taken. On the other hand, there is the lack of action that has been taken by people in power. Then too, the people that have been hurt do nothing to make things better. That's why I like to write this column. Besides making you laugh, maybe you can think of ways to enrich your life and the lives of others.

Let's look at some issues. For example, at the same time corporate business has handed the responsibility for pension plans over to the government, they are awarding huge increases in executive salaries and giving them beautiful pension plans. Now

The Soup of Life

the government will give the laborers 50 to 75 percent of their pensions. Guess who's going to pay for this? The taxpayers. Is this fair?

If someone takes your money and won't give it back, this used to be called stealing. Or is it stealing when it's a small amount and good business if it's a huge amount?

I can't help but think that if this were happening in Italy there would be a big strike and outcry. The Italians strike at the drop of a hat. I remember the first time Russ and I went to Italy in 1963, we had to change our plans because the airlines went on strike. We had to go from Palermo to Naples by boat. They put all the women in one section and the men were put in another section. One couple had just gotten married that day!

Now let's return to the pension fiasco. Who's to blame for this dilemma? The administration and the workers who have both allowed it. Where does accountability step in? I understand the pension benefit guarantee corporation that was handling the pension fund lost a lot of money in the 90s when the stock market collapsed. So much for the security of securities. So they handed their problem to the government.

What happened to "government of the people, by the people, for the people?" Lincoln would turn over in his grave! He wanted his people to never perish. Are we going to let it erode little by little?

I like programs that are for all the people (not on a percentage basis). For example, every year in Alaska the profits from the oil business are divided equally among every citizen of Alaska. I've been told it goes from $1,000 to $4,000 for each member of the family. Can you imagine what the impact this has on the economy? Good for you, Alaska! Can you think of any ideas New York State can implement? Put on your thinking caps!

Margaret Valone

Character Development

There were different reactions to my kindergarten story. One woman said, "You must have been a holy terror." No, I just couldn't cut out a rabbit. I still can't unless it is already formed. Many thought it was a good plan coming from a 4-year-old, I don't know if it was a result of this incident but I hate swearing. I hate to hear it and I certainly don't use it. I remember one day when I was waiting to catch a bus to Dunkirk to go to work (ancient history) there were some high school girls waiting for the bus, too. Every other word was a swear word and they were using the f-word to boot. They sounded worse than boys. If only they knew how they were degrading themselves. This is a good time to check yourself out and your family out. Discuss it at the dining room table. Really, you have to nip it in the bud in the home.

Anyway, there were a lot of lessons to be learned by that story. While we're talking about flaws in our character, let's talk about greed. I'm sure if we made a list of all the evils in this world, we'd find greed and power at the top of the list or close. It starts with trying to keep up with the Joneses and even though Dan Jones was one of our son's best friends, we never tried to keep up with the Joneses. What do you have to do to like yourself? Keep yourself clean in body, mind and soul. Do for others whenever you can and however you can. These are just simple things that you are in control of.

I'm remembering a story when Dan was around 10 years old. He found a wallet on Main Street in front of McEntarfer's Pharmacy. It had more than $100 in it. Wow! He started to go into the drugstore and a woman came out and he asked her if she had

The Soup of Life

lost her wallet. She checked and she had. She took the wallet, got into her Cadillac and drove off. "Gee mom, she didn't even say thanks." "That's OK, Dan, you did the right thing and I'm, proud of you. Dad will be proud, too, when I tell him." We were happy. Do you see how many things can be learned in the home? We build relationships there too which are carried over with friends and people in authority.

Someone sent me this. "Subject: Enough. Recently overheard: a father and daughter in their last moments together. They had announced her departure and standing near the security gate, they hugged and he said, 'I love you. I wish you enough.' She in turn said, 'Daddy, our life together has been more than enough. Your, love is all I ever needed. I wish you enough, too, Daddy.' They kissed and she left. He walked over toward the window where I was seated. Standing there I could see he wanted and needed to cry. I tried not to intrude on his privacy, but he welcomed me in by asking, 'Did you ever say goodbye to someone knowing it would be forever?'"

"Yes, I have", I replied.

Saying that brought back memories I had of expressing my love and appreciation for all my dad had done for me. Recognizing that his days were limited, I took the time to tell him face-to-face how much he meant to me. So I knew what this man was experiencing. "Forgive me for asking, but why is this a forever goodbye?" I asked.

"I am old and she lives much too far away. I have challenges ahead and the reality is, the next trip back would be for my funeral", he said.

"When you were saying goodbye, I heard you say, 'I wish you enough.' May I ask what that means?"

He began to smile. "That's a wish that has been handed down from other generations. My parents used to say it to everyone." He paused for a moment and looking up as if trying to remember in detail, he smiled even more. "When we said 'I wish you enough', we were wanting the other person to have a life filled with just

Margaret Valone

enough good things to sustain them", he continued and then turning toward me he shared the following as if he were reciting it from memory.

"I wish you enough sun to keep your attitude bright.

I wish you enough rain to appreciate the sun more.

I wish you enough happiness to keep your spirit alive.

I wish you enough pain so that the smallest joys in life appear much bigger.

I wish you enough gain to satisfy your wanting.

I wish you enough loss to appreciate all that you possess.

I wish you enough 'Hellos' to get you through the final 'Goodbye'."

Then, tears in his eyes, he walked away.

Family and friends, I wish you enough.

I'm sure this father and daughter have a very special relationship. Just remember: today's oak is yesterday's nut that held its ground. Middle age is when you choose your cereal for its fiber, not the toy.

The Soup of Life

Journalism Matters

On TV, I watched Bill Moyers address a teacher's group on the subject "Journalism Matters". I'm so wound up I have to tell you about it. First of all, I had just finished watching the pre-season Buffalo Bills game against the New Orleans Saints. I didn't feel like going to bed, so I "accidentally" found the program on C-SPAN, which I rarely watch. Am I glad I listened because we, the nation, need to know what's going on in the world of news dissemination. He said, "Reporting is the food chain of democracy." And I'll add my opinion that we are being fed a lot of garbage! Or our food is being withheld. Moyers talked about what's going on in newspapers today. Some are losing money. Reporting the truth is expensive. People, big companies, and CEOs will pay big money to keep the truth from us, but the public is the only one who can insist on good, truthful reporting and be willing to pay for it. I know we complain about prices going up, but what will happen if our newspapers and radio commentators are gagged? Where will we get the truth? He said since 1980, CBS has cut 60 percent of its staff and many of the reporters today are being poorly paid.

He told many stories. I don't know how many listen to Rush Limbaugh, but here's what he had to say about the reporting of the American soldiers who raped and killed some Iraqi women. "There were words to the effect that it shouldn't have been made a big deal of by some media. To report it was unpatriotic. They were just blowing off steam." Moyers said he knew others who blew off steam (a lot of hot air). They are called "radio talk show commentators."

He discussed the recent purchase of the Wall Street Journal by

Mr. Murdoch. He has big investments in China. He controls Fox network, among many others that treat the public as consumers, not citizens. I have a question - aren't monopolies no longer prohibited? Who defines a monopoly?

One of the things that makes this country such a great country is that in a democracy, we are afforded the privilege of disagreeing with our rulers or, should I say, "representatives." If our information is controlled, our senses will become dull and our way of life will die. I think if I remember correctly, it was Voltaire who said, "I may not agree with what you say, but I'll fight to the death for your right to say it." Now if my memory fails me, it's OK by me, I'm not a perfectionist. It's the principle of free speech that I embrace.

Moyers told this story about some children who were playing in the chicken coop. They saw a barn snake and ran so fast and hard that they broke off part of the barn and hurt themselves. The mother of one of the boys came out to see what had happened. Then she told them that that kind of snake is harmless.

"I know," said one of the boys, "but sometimes they scare you so much, you hurt yourself." We have nothing to fear but fear itself," President Roosevelt said.

Boy, if that story isn't food for thought! It drives home the fact that fear can have far-reaching effects. I see politicians using the "fear card" all the time and play the "what if" game. Let's not be duped. We have enough real situations all around us to handle that we can't afford to play those games.

I see state and federal governments arguing over the dumbest things just to keep the opposition from doing something productive that they can brag about in the next campaign. Why can't they do it together and then both brag? Another word I have for you stubborn, nearsighted politicians is this - if you can't do what you'd like to do, then do what you can do! You can start by telling your constituents the truth and then ask for their help. If you do it together, it will happen faster and then you can like each other and yourselves better.

The Soup of Life

Why couldn't you tell someone on the other side of the aisle, "That's a good idea, Let's do it." Then maybe he'll reciprocate for you. So you think I'm being naive? How would you know if you don't try it?

I believe in giving credit where credit is due. Being appreciative can start new, meaningful relationships. Don't be afraid to be the first to break the ice.

I'll leave you with this last thought Bill Moyers had – "Contrary to what Wall Street says, time is more valuable than money."

I just happened to think of this - why do we always say; "spend time?" When we spend money, we always have something to show for it. We also should reap from our time spent. And just think - you're in charge of that time! Wow!

Have a good Friday.

Waxing Political

It's interesting to hear about all the possible candidates who want to run for office. Do you ever daydream about the platform you would run on? I do. Here are some of the things I would run on.

First of all, I'd make the campaigning time no more than three months. Why? I hate to hear the same things repeated over and over again for one-and-a-half years. It would be less time for big lies and distortions. It would cost less. The Supreme Court should have voted to limit the amount of money a candidate could use on the campaign. Each candidate would have equal opportunity. As it is now, a candidate has two choices - either he is rich enough to pay for all expenses or he has to find people who will sponsor him and then he will be in their pocket and can't be his own person. I don't trust a rich man to run because he is used to being rich and he'll want to get richer and richer. They can never have enough.

Do you remember what Rockefeller said when he was asked, "How many millions are enough?" His answer was. "One million more than you have." Even he knew that and admitted it.

Our government should be a government of the people, by the people and for the people, but it's not anymore. Now we are run by a small group of moneyed people who concentrate on making more profit for themselves. Wars make some people richer and richer. Peace may not make us richer, but we wouldn't be poorer. Drug trafficking makes many people richer. That's why a country that says they are the most powerful nation in the world can't control the drug problem. They can't or don't control our illegal immigrant problem because too many people are making money on these illegal immigrants. What did you think when Lou Dobbs of CNN, who attacked illegal immigration every night, was exposed for using them to take care of his estates? (Notice the "s" on estates). While I'm on this subject, many of the immigrants are being held in jail either because they are illegal or they have committed crimes. Each year they are in prison costs between $40,000 to 45,000 each and some states even say more.

You want to cut down on our debt? Release them and drop them off at home. I feel sorry for them but we can't afford them. Nor can we afford giving them health care and free education. Will someone give us the true costs? Can we afford to do all this for them and at the same time talk about doing away with Medicare and Social Security, which will require a person to work until they are 70?

Let's examine our past. When drinking alcohol was illegal, it didn't work. Now that it's legal I can't see how it is ruining our country. Drunk drivers are arrested because they are dangerous. Why couldn't we do the same with drugs? We could make a lot of money. Why not try it? If it doesn't work, then try something else. Getting back to prison, did you know that even though the U.S. is 5 percent of the world population, we have 25 percent of the world's prisoners and we call ourselves a free country? We have less freedom and our expenses are enormous.

We're consolidating and closing schools. Why can't we do the same with prisons? Where are our values? So many "good people" only care about punishment, but that is negative thinking. When they get out of prison sometimes they have become hardened prisoners, they have not been trained to work so they either go back to prison or on welfare. We are shooting ourselves in the foot. I would take a positive approach.

Getting back to my platform, I would put a ceiling on holding office for eight years and then take a break for eight years. Funny, just after I wrote this, I saw a clip of Harry Truman advocating allowing only two terms of office which is eight years for senators. So I guess I'm not out of line.

Do you remember when we had the last oil embargo the speed limit on the Thruway was 55 mph? That rate saves gas, saves money and saves lives, but who cares?

Wouldn't it be nice if national holidays were the same for everybody?

I probably could find more things, but what for? I'd never win and neither would anyone else with this platform. How can we ask our representatives to do things that would help us and sometimes hurt them? That's like asking the wolf to watch the hen house.

Well, I've said my piece. You don't have to call me or write to me because I'm not running, but I hope I gave you a lot of food for thought. Munch on it. It's not fattening. Ask yourself, "What would my platform be?" Just remember, if you're not part of the solution, you're part of the problem.

The Soup of Life

Reflecting on Our Nation's Problems

In this column I'm going to vent many emotions. I'm sad about the way our country has lost its image to the world, especially to us. We have lost our reputation, our respect and most of all, our identity.

Our representatives have lost my respect. They don't care about the people. They just care about being reelected or elected and lining their pockets. Isn't it ironic that the rich, the Republican party, are adamant about giving to the government but are raising umpteen dollars for the campaign? Obama would do the same, but he doesn't have the background, so he's going after the Latino vote. He even wants to pass a bill giving children of illegal immigrants free college! That's crazy. The cost of education is going up for our kids, and they are going to get their education for free? No way.

Now I come from an immigrant family, but before they could come, they had to have a sponsor. My father's sister was married to John Joy of Water Street and had to sponsor them for four years. Now if these people don't have relatives here, why not let their employers sponsor them? Find a way, but not at the taxpayers' expense! Let's get real.

What's wrong with our country? We're so arrogant, prideful and money-hungry! Where is our humility and love?

9/11 proved to us that we were not invincible. The enemy struck. So what was our natural instinct? We would rebuild and make the new building bigger and better. We were disdainful. This reaction is par for the course.

I'm reading a book called "The Harbinger" by Jonathan Cahn. In this book, he compares the downfall of Israel in the Old Testament to the coming of the downfall of America. The similarities are incredible! It makes you think. We definitely are on the road to destruction and what can we do about it? We can change, turn around and live by our old standards of morality.

Let us start in the home. Let parents be parents. Teach your children respect. Make them use clean language. No profanity, no sassing back. Teach them to have respect for their elders, for their teachers, for church people and for friends. Love them a lot and act accordingly. Praise them, dress them properly and be an example of what you want them to be. Teach them the rewards of living clean, keeping the house clean and themselves clean. Others will approve of them and they will have good self images.

The schools must continue with these principles and add to them. Their experiences at school and the attitudes of the teachers and their experiences will add up to make them happy campers. If the majority of the people have these good experiences, we will have a good society. We have lost so much of this and we have to get it back.

Now the church should play a big part in doing the same things and much more. Society would be much better off if they used the same principles. So many of them are the same! Let's forget the labels. If the principles work to make us better people and happier people, we would be foolish not to apply them to our lives. I always remember my brother-in-law, Angelo. He was my favorite. He used to love to tease me and act like he didn't like me. Like he would say things like, "Here are some cookies. Pass them around but not to Margaret."

I would say, "That's O.K. I like you and liking you makes me feel good, so I'll keep that good feeling."

You see, we have choices. Make good choices and you'll be rewarded with good feelings.

I have no confidence in our congressional system and I wish there were enough voters to let them know they have no confidence in them and are going to hold back their votes until they know they are going to work for the good of our country and not just concentrating on making their opponents look bad. Remember, you reap what you sow. We are all farmers in this field of life.

Margaret Valone

Sharing Your Thoughts

When I first started writing this column I had no idea how it would go and where it would go. I had no theme. I guess if I had to give it a title it would be, *How to Get the Most Out of Life*. The response has been exciting, even the men look for it.

I've always wanted to be a networker. I got a taste of it in the beauty salon. A customer had a problem and the people in the beauty salon, including hairdressers, had information. Sometimes, all you need is a start and then it gains momentum. Well, this is how the column has evolved. I'll give you some examples. First, I received a call from a girlfriend telling me about a wonderful service given to people who need transportation for medical reasons. She sent me the brochure. It's called Wings Flights of Hope. It provides free flights for all medical patients and our troops. Sometimes the patients are children or even adults who need family to accompany them for appointments. Everyone will fly free. The only requirement is all patients must be able to get in and out of the aircraft with little or no assistance.

Wings will fly anywhere and at any time. When every minute counts, for example if patients are receiving an organ transplant and every minute counts, they will fly you day or night. They also help in times of natural disaster. These pilots are all volunteers. They never get paid. They even contribute the gas.

This service is made possible by individuals and businesses. Call 1-866-61-WINGS (1-866-619-4647) or www.wingsflight.org. Thank you, Joyce, for sharing this helpful service. Doesn't it warm

The Soup of Life

your heart to find out there are such caring people just waiting to be of service?

Then I had a call from a man in Portland who told me he responds to all the junk mail he gets. He takes a marker and writes "cancel" right across the top of the letter and sends it back. Some of them have gotten the message and he gets less junk mail. Thank you for your input.

Next, I received a letter from a reader telling me what would happen to Noah today if he were given the charge to make the ark. It's really funny if it weren't so true. Here it is, entitled *If It Happened Today*:

> And the Lord spoke to Noah and said, 'In six months I'm going to make it rain, cover the whole planet with water and destroy all the evil people. I command you to build an ark to my specifications and use it to house two of every living thing.' And the Lord said, 'Be sure to have it done in six months, or learn to swim for a very long time.'
>
> Six months passed, the rain began to fall, the Lord saw Noah weeping in the front yard. And no ark to be seen. 'Noah', shouted the Lord, 'Where is the ark?'
>
> 'Lord, please forgive me,' begged Noah, 'I did my best but there were problems. First I had to get a building permit for the ark, but your plans didn't meet code. So I hired an engineer to redraw the plans, then I got into a big fight over whether I needed a fire sprinkler system. Then my neighbor objected, claiming I was violating zoning laws, by constructing an ark in my front yard. I had to get a variance from the planning board. Then I had to satisfy the local carpenter's union to show that I would hire only union help at state prevailing wages. Then I had problems getting enough wood for the ark, because there was a ban on cutting trees to save the spotted owl. I had to convince the U.S. Fish and Wildlife

Service that I needed the wood to save the owls. But then they wouldn't let me catch any, so, no owls.

When I started to gather up the animals, two of each, the animal rights groups objected to only taking two. Then I had to assure the EPA there would not be any noxious gas emissions, and then notified me I couldn't complete the ark, without filing an environment impact statement, on your proposed land flooding. They didn't take kindly to their not having jurisdiction over a supreme being. Then the Army Corps of Engineers wanted a map of the proposed flood plain, so I sent them the globe.

Right now, I'm still trying to resolve a complaint from the Equal Employment Opportunity Commission over how many Croations to hire. Now the IRS has seized all my assets, claiming I'm trying to avoid paying taxes by leaving the country. And I just got a notice from the state about owing them some kind of 'use' tax.

'I really don't think I can finish the ark for another five years', Noah wailed.

Just then, the sky cleared, the sun shone, Noah looked up and smiled.

'You mean you're not going to destroy the Earth?' Noah asked hopefully.

'No', the Lord sadly said. 'The government already has'."

John, I thank you so much for this commentary. It's clever, but it's so sad because we're killing ourselves with all these controls. How much freedom do we really have in our country? We should be vigilant. We fought so hard to get it but we can't take it for granted.

If you have any principles or experiences you'd like share, please feel free to contact me at (904) 679-4772.

The Soup of Life

Voice Your Opinion

I recently received my gas bill. It was $247. I couldn't believe it! The weather has been mild. I put my thermostat down to 60 degrees at night, keep it between 68 and 70 degrees during the day and wear a layered look. What else can I do?

I called up the company and told him just what I have written. This bill is bigger than last year when the weather was colder. I apologized. I wasn't mad at him; I was just upset. He said he was used to it. He heard it all day long. I asked him if the price had gone up. He said that no, it was just what the government allowed.

After I hung up, that word "allowed" kept ringing in my ear. Sure, it's allowed because we allow it! Until the lobbies for the energy people are stopped and all the control they have is broken, we are at their mercy and it is all our fault. We allow it! We get what we deserve for not protesting loud enough or often enough. If we did it all at the same time, they'd have to hear us!

If you agree with what I'm saying, cut out the column and send it to the representatives. Don't just send to the ones who agree with you, but to those who have to be persuaded. If you need addresses, I have them.

Now is the time to get vocal. Put the pressure on the Democrats. They have done a lot of talking, but it's the action that counts. And don't tell me talk is cheap. Every time the wrong people talk it costs us money! Don't forget: there's another election coming soon.

I have found it encouraging to find a lot of independent

thinking going on in Congress and also among the voters. So many times I have wished that we could throw them all out and start all over. I have been involved in boards and politics and I know how hard it is to get things done. I don't think like a lot of people.

For example, when I was on the Fredonia School Board and several teachers were going to be released because of lack of funds, I thought the teachers would have taken a small cut to keep their friends in. Unfortunately, it doesn't work like that in any occupation. We have been brainwashed that success means more and more. The word "enough" is not in the vocabulary. But, I'll tell you, if you get past that point, you can have such peace!

Recently I wrote to a senator pointing out to him that the leadership could turn this country around by setting the example. They should take a cut. Instead of voting. themselves a big raise, they should take a small raise or no raise. Wouldn't that be refreshing?

I can hear some of you saying "dream on", but it could happen. Do I think I'm going to make it with my letter? Of course not! But if enough of you send the same letter, they might listen. I'm not responsible for what you do or don't do, or what the Senate does, but I am responsible for my actions or lack thereof.

What Happened to America?

I was brought up in a family that were educators, businessmen and women and all were very political-minded but we were very different politicians. When we read in the Constitution "Of the people, by the people and for the people" we read that politicians were supposed to give service, not line their own pockets with money and search for power. Do our kind of politicians still exist?

I came across a list of things I was interested in. I've always wanted to protect Social Security money. I still want to eliminate lobbyists. They buy influence and then our congressmen are indebted to them. Why can't our congressmen get things done that are good for the people in-general? That's their job. The pork that is dished out is just like the lobbyists.

How do you feel about limiting the number of congressional terms allowed continuously? They can go back. Should we limit the age of congressmen? How old? Do you think Supreme Court judges should be for life? They can be lax in their jobs; it gives too much power.

Let's look at the immigrant problem in Florida. Some places you can't buy what you want unless you speak Spanish.

Shouldn't English be our first language? Shouldn't all immigrants be treated equally? The word illegal means it's not legal. If we need workers from other countries, they should have working papers that express their rights and their limitations. Some illegals get benefits our own people don't get. This is wrong. Where are our leaders? Who is going to help our new candidates when they get into office?

We have lost our image. We have always been good Christians helping the needy to help themselves be solvent. This way money spent is an investment, not an extravagance.

This should be good business, not a political football. Where are our leaders who can change a standing policy? Are you for helping the needy or helping yourself? Is money the common denominator? Is there only one party? Oh, they may have different names, but are they still one party?

How can we save money on transportation especially now that gas prices are so ridiculous? Are people still car pooling? Are manufacturers making smaller cars? Are speed limits being lowered? We can save a lot of money going back to 50 miles or 60 miles per hour. It might reduce our accident rates, too. Why don't we think of the need, of all people involved in interest groups?

Challenge the voters, all voters, to make a better life for everyone. We need volunteers in all areas. Do you know how much money we can save? Let's motivate the rich to give freely instead of making them feel we are holding them up. We have a few millionaires who are giving freely. Why not more of them? That good feeling of being helpful is the same for the poor who give and the rich that give. We should all praise anyone who gives whether it's a small amount or a large donation!

Where's the America we used to know? I was so proud to be an American when we traveled abroad! They loved us. Except three years ago, a Roman lady spit in one of our traveler's face when she identified herself as an American. Where has our image gone? How can we get it back? The principles we have always clung to made us loved throughout history. Our principles started with our Constitution. We've lost our image! Let's get it back! In our family, we were always taught that our reputation was priceless. It was to be valued. Let's start with the families. Make it a priority in the schools, the churches and our society. It's not too late. You have to give respect to get respect.

All this bickering in politics is putting us down. Let's try to outdo each other on all the good we can do - and I don't mean spending money!

It's Time to Take Action

I never know where I am going to get new material for this column. Last week I went to a funeral luncheon. I sat with strangers. One woman and I were very compatible. She was a retired school teacher. She told me something I hadn't heard before. She said the biggest problem with education was trying to get kids to come to school. They have no respect for teachers or education.

When I hear the word "respect", my ears perk up. Respect is the foundation of all relationships. If the students have no respect for education, neither do the parents. Let's stop and consider this. This is a biggie. Parents have to take their responsibility to get their children to school very seriously. No "ifs" or "ands" about it. You go to school every day. You listen to the teacher. You learn the material every day. You respect the teacher. If you are disrespectful, you will, be punished at home.

Education is priceless. This is a three-way street - parents and children - children and teachers. All three work together as a team.

She also said the teachers were interested in their paychecks too much. The union kept pushing for more and more money instead of making sure the students were learning. I think this is reflected in the drop of ratings our students have in world ratings. What happened? We used to be first.

We talked about the fact that just because your child graduates from college doesn't mean he or she will get a job. As a matter of fact, she said to me, "Everybody talks about your generation and how good it was. But the government provided for our soldiers to go to college."

The baby boomers didn't have the same opportunities their generation had. Some of them went to college. Some didn't. Not all of those who graduated found jobs in their fields. In our generation people worked in one job for life. Her generation changed jobs, several or many times. Now she has a daughter that is graduating this year. Now her daughter is fearful about finding a job. She owes a lot to the college. Are college graduates much better off? She gave me food for thought.

Then in Sunday's paper, there was a big column written by Warren Beyer. I hope you saved it. I had to call him up and thank him for a lesson in American history. Then I found out he had been a history teacher.

Beyer says there's a spirit of anger in this country. I hope he's right. There has been spirit of lethargy that drives me crazy. Maybe anger will lead to demanding the spirit to take action: The lower socio-economic classes have lost their faith that things will get better. The middle class has lost their life savings, but the upper socio-economic class has it made. They are protected. They take no responsibility to pay their fair share. And they are getting away with it.

Look at what Wall Street, the banks, and the government have done to our economy. They sold worthless mortgages to the public, they altered their books, they gave out bad investments and no one went to jail. How can this be? I guess we're saying if you're rich enough you can get away with anything. How come the CEOs gave themselves big raises while the lower classes took cuts?

Beyer pointed out how these rich people are using our roads to deliver their products, they are protected by our police departments, our fire departments, they are protected by a military system the taxpayers provide. They enjoy all these privileges that the taxpayers are providing for them and they do not pay one cent in taxes, They also enjoy the freedoms to do business in this country and do not pay their fair share of taxes to use these things which taxpayers paid for. How do they get away with it? When do we say enough is enough? Those who don't want to pay their fair share do not a deserve a piece of the dream.

People who have power will not give up their power. It has to be taken from them. Does this mean we have to take power from our own people? Of course, greed and power go together.

No one seems to have any answers on how to make these greedy, powerful people pay for what they are doing to our country. Make the courts make them pay with time and money.

Our whole system of government needs to be revised. Only the rich and the good old boys can afford to run for Congress or president. This is not democratic. Every candidate would be given the same amount of money for his campaign. Then the candidate will have to run on his own merit. There should be only three months to campaign. All this money spent on advertising would be limited. Sell your message. Don't use all that time and money on slandering each other. Of course, that takes the profit out of publicity. Too bad.

These are my ideas. Let's take the muck and shame out of the race.

There's one other young man whom I respect and I asked him if there was any hope for our country.

He didn't hesitate. He said the answer is in II Chronicles 7:14 which says "If my people who are called by my name, shall humble themselves, and pray and seek my face, and turn from their wicked ways, then will I hear from heaven, and will forgive their sin, and I will heal their land."

He went on to say there are 50 churches in this area and they are all divided. He blames the churches. There's enough blame to go around for everybody.

I want to draw something to your attention. Warren Beyer believes that men who. have gained power (includes wealth, greed, pride)-will never give it up. It has to be taken from them.

Now in II Chronicles 7:14 it says "If my people will humble

themselves". Isn't it strange that the Bible takes the opposite word from the world's view? The Bible says we have to become humble. Jesus was the epitome of humbleness. But in our world we seek to be proud. We're proud Americans, we're proud of our big cars, our mansions, etc. There's joy in humility. Another comparison is humility gives and pride takes. Do we have the answers and we're ignoring them?

Isn't it strange how these three different people were thrown into my path in a week? I'm grateful to each of them.

The Soup of Life

There Is No Such Thing as Failure

I get the idea for this column through many sources. Sometimes I receive medical reports, sometimes readers will ask a question or give me answers. Sometimes it's current events that set me off. Sometimes it's philosophical thinking and sometimes it's about life in general, things that bring pleasures and things that cause problems. If we can help each other on any level and we don't, that's very sad.

Sometimes I think about the regrets people have when they die. I wonder if the regrets were for the things they had done or regrets for the things they either never did or never finished. If you're afraid of change or of failure, you will die with many regrets. Don't be afraid. There's no such thing as failure. If nothing else, you learned you were wrong and can make corrections which will bring you joy.

In the mail today I learned there are four things you can't recover:
1. The stone - after the throw.
2. The word - after it's said.
3. The occasion - after it's missed.
4. The time - after it's gone.

The first one - after you throw stones - to me doesn't literally mean throwing a pebble but rather after you said something ugly about someone. Sometimes I think we should add "You can't unsee something you saw." We should be very careful what we watch and we should be very careful about what people see when they look at us.

Margaret Valone

The first two were actions and the last two were lack of action. All refer to time and time is life. It's the most precious gift we have. I've always tried to make wise use of my time, If I had saved money like I saved time, I'd be a millionaire. But by using my time wisely, I've had a good life. If you're dissatisfied with your life, you can change it today. And I don't mean your watch!

Let's compare earthly thinking with the heavenly kingdom. Our governments maintain power by wars which are costly both physically and monetarily. While the heavenly kingdom is founded by the Prince of Peace. Sounds great to me - just the opposite.

Have you ever thought much about seeds and planting? You'd better think of it because the cost of food is getting unbelievable. I'm urging everybody to plant home gardens. If you don't have room, ask a neighbor or a farmer to let you plant an area.

Let's think about seeds and the lessons we can learn from seeds. Have you ever noticed after you plant a fruit tree that the seeds are in the fruit and you can plant them to get more fruit? And the fruit always replaces itself. Apple seeds do not reproduce peach trees.

There are a couple more observations we can make. When you plant wheat, you have to throw the seeds out. If you hang on to them, they will die. I think this teaches us we should not try to keep things. By throwing the seed out, they reproduce and give us abundances. We can equate that to giving. I love to give to that organization in Africa that helps women go into business for themselves. They receive a small amount of money. They make something and sell it. Then they give back a little and they get more, They increase their businesses and save some of the money. Why couldn't all agencies operate on good common sense like that?

Have you ever noticed that most seeds have to be planted and die before they can produce? You plant a seed and it doesn't grow up a seed. It is transformed into a vegetable or fruit or flower or a tree. We take all these things for granted but the world is so beautifully made, we have to see the orderliness of creation.

So far we've talked about physical seeding. Now let's talk about

The Soup of Life

abstract planting. We need to sow seeds of compassion, sympathy, kindness and love because we reap what we sow. Life can be so enjoyable and easy. Let's get smart.

I have a surprise for you. This letter came to me from Bill Schank who is in prison in Alabama. Do you remember a few weeks ago I wrote about forgiveness? Have you forgiven Bill Schank? I have because if Christ has forgiven him, who am I not to forgive? You know in the Lord's Prayer, Christ wrote, "and forgive us our sins as we forgive others." That means in direct proportion to as we forgive others. So that means we are really praying condemnation on ourselves if we are unforgiving.

I look forward to Bill's letters. I'm his "Ma Margaret" and he blesses me all the time. I'd like to close with this poem written by one of the workers at the prison:

> "I'm sorry for what I did
> It was a terrible thing to do
> My frustration got the best of me
> And I guess the stress did, too
> I promise I will never do
> What I did that depressing night it's just that I was sad
> Because my family and I had a fight.
> That fight had pushed me over the limit
> And I did not know what to do
> If I had really been thinking hard enough
> I would have turned to you.
> If I ever get off that track again
> I'll pray that you will help
> It gets hard sometimes in the world today
> And I often just think of myself.
> I never thought that what I did would make others feel that bad
> And when I think of what I did now
> It really makes me sad.
> Sad for all the pain I'd caused
> And for all those shed tears
> But I will not ever do it again
> Because I have you to calm my fears
> You will calm my fears and

Margaret Valone

Everything else including any strife
I learned that many years ago
When I allowed you in my life."

    I thought the poem was very appropriate because this is the Easter season. I was very impressed by this man's poem. I would never have guessed it came from a man in prison. It just goes to prove anyone can change.

The Soup of Life

The Pros and Cons of Gambling

Let's talk about gambling. The word itself has a negative connotation. The only two situations where gambling has a positive upscale connotation are Wall Street and farming. Yes, investing in Wall Street is gambling. I know because this week I lost $2,000. If my investments made money, I'd share them with you, but you don't need to know about my losers.

I always say if you're going to play the slot machines, blackjack, or shoot dice, don't gamble more than you can afford to lose. The same principle holds true for Wall Street.

Now let's look at the farmers. We are blessed to have so many that are willing to feed us at great risks to themselves. Let's face it, they work so hard getting the land ready. They till the soil, plant the seeds, nurture those seeds, and then they have to pray that nature won't wipe them out. Too much sun, not enough sun, too much water, not enough water, and the timing for these needs has to be perfect!

My father used to get so angry when people tried to bargain with the farmers over their produce. They deserve every cent they can get. If they counted the hours they put in, they are probably working for minimum wage. But we respect them.

Now I want to touch on how government manipulates our minds. Whenever our political leaders want to keep our minds off of what they want to do, they divert our thoughts to our blind spots. Unfortunately, we are a one-issue people. Oh, we don't all have the same issue, but there are some issues that push our buttons.

For example, I think most of us value our freedoms, especially our freedom of choice. That is a God-given right. We may choose Him or choose not to choose Him and of course, that's what democracy is all about. We have to choose what's best for all the people, not a selective few. If we choose to keep our eyes on all the moral issues and close our eyes to the economic issues, we are not being wise. I think if I can keep my morals intact, I am doing well. That is the only area where I have control. It's the only area where each of us has control. If each of us will work on this it will become evident in our society. We can influence more people by being good role models than any legislation.

On top of that it will leave your minds open to other things that are going on. We must be vigilant and inform our representatives how we feel. We're so proud to live in our nation where we elect our representatives and then they never hear from us! That's not fair to them. If we never tell them how we feel, we can't get mad if they only vote on how they feel. Let's exercise our rights!

Defining a Gift

What is a gift? If I give the students upstairs a spaghetti dinner and then ask them to clear off the porch and wash my windows, is this a gift? Or if I tell someone I'll give her a haircut or a perm if she'll clean my house, is this a gift? Does a gift have strings attached? Not if it's a true gift.

Then there's the obligation that goes with a gift. If someone gives you an unexpected gift, do you feel you have to return a gift of the same value? How often do we do these things? Then there's this situation that I just love: you give someone a gift and she says, "I know so and so who would just love this. I'll give it to her." No, lady, I gave it to her. Come to think of it, she gave it up, so I guess we both gave it to her.

Now let's talk about our natural gifts. Don't tell me you don't have any because "God don't make no junk". Some people's gifts are very visible. Talents in acting, dancing, singing, or playing musical instruments. Look at all the paintings and sculpture work in clay or wood. These are all given much exposure, but they are small categories.

Now we have the caring gifts. The doctors and nurses give of themselves and their talents daily as they care for their patients. The medications are provided through the skills of medical science. You may consider eating establishments as businesses, but they not only feed people, but provide an atmosphere where their clients can relax. This is a gift. And of course, most mothers do this at home.

What about good teachers? If a teacher has the gift of teaching, he or she can bring the outside world into their classrooms. They can instill a thirst for learning that will never die. What a gift and privilege. I forgot to mention the arts of speaking and writing. People gifted in these areas move the public to do good and evil.

We must not overlook the precious gift of being a homemaker or good parents. You don't have to earn a degree or take a crash course. A loving heart is priceless. With a loving heart comes peace, joy, good deeds, caring hands, smiling faces, laughter, encouragement, comfort, wisdom, etc. How can you measure the worth of all that? Fortunately, we fully appreciate the attributes given to us by God as much as those earned from man's standards.

Many times I ask the questions: What do I have to do to like myself? To respect myself? To accept myself? Do you ask yourself these questions? The answers are all within us. Look for them. Find them and use them! I figure I have the gifts of hospitality, giving, encouragement, and writing. The beauty part is I don't have to study, I don't have to be a fashion plate, I don't have to set a quota. I will just relax and as the opportunities arise, I will react.

I think it is timely that we talk about our gifts, because we need to use them now more than ever before. There's so much going on in the world today that is very frightening. Unfortunately, there's so little we can do to change things, but there is so much we can do here. First, we have to have an awareness of all the gifts we have that can bring comfort and joy to others. There's no enemy holding you back, except yourself. You have the power to eliminate that enemy. Do what you can and enlighten others to do what they can. Spread the good news. We need it.

Isn't this a good Friday?

A Healthy Serving of Advice

I have some good news for people who have cancer and those that want to prevent cancer. Research has shown us simple ways to reduce our cancer risk. Take note:
1. Avoid tobacco products.
2. Eat more fruit and vegetables in your diet.

Here are some recommendations: real teas such as green, white, and red are rich in flavonoids, powerful antioxidants, which help the body by protecting it against diseases by counteracting the harmful effects of cell damage from free radicals. Ketchup and tomato sauce contain another powerful antioxidant called lycopene, which may help lower the risk of developing cancer.
1. Foods rich in vitamin C such as orange juice and other citrus fruits may help prevent oral, esophageal, lung, stomach and colon cancers.
2. There are some vegetables such as cabbage, broccoli, brussell sprouts, and turnips that may help prevent against colon, stomach and respiratory cancers. In general, include fruits and vegetables in your diets. Increase fiber intake.
3. Avoid excess sun, wear sunscreen of SPF 30 or higher.
4. Limit alcohol intake.
5. Maintain a healthy weight.
6. Know the warning signs for common cancers and do self-exams, know your family history (medical).

Here are some tips to help cancer survivors live a better life:
1. Eat three balanced meals a day with a small snack between meals.
2. Have dried fruit as a healthy snack.

3. Avoid snacking all day in place of meals: this will lower your appetite.
4. Cook a home-cooked meal. The smell and seeing others eat will help the appetite.
5. Include proteins and starches in meals. The body needs calories and you will feel stronger.
6. Drink a fruit smoothie or vegetable juice between meals to provide needed vitamins.

One thing that wasn't mentioned in this information is simply this: keep a happy outlook. Just last night, I was reminiscing with a friend of mine on all the fun we had in the waiting room while we were waiting for our radiation treatments. There wasn't a sourpuss in the room: That was nine years ago and we're both doing fine. I've had cancer operations twice. I can use those experiences to encourage people who are going through treatment. I welcome two heart operations, two cancer operations, and two deaths in my family; my son and my husband, because all these experiences make me a qualified person to help people who are mourning. You don't remember you experienced these trails, but dwell on all the joys you've had after each experience. All in all, each of us has had a purposeful life.

Here's some advice specifically for women:
1. To find heart problems before you have symptoms there is a 64-slice CT scanner. The scan takes 5 minutes and is painless.
2. All low-fat dairy products can lower your blood pressure.
3. Fill up on whole fruits and veggies to help protect your body from forming cancer cells.
4. Vitamin E may help keep artery walls clean, which will help cardiovascular problems.
5. With women, heart attacks feel like indigestion or throat discomfort.
6. Thanks to Herceptin, up to 84 percent of women with breast cancer are reportedly now recurrence-free!

Here are six ways to reduce risk of Alzheimer's:
1. Bring down high blood pressure and high cholesterol.
2. Exercise 30 minutes at least five days a week.
3. If obese, lose weight and start slowly.

The Soup of Life

4. Stay mentally and socially active.
5. Exercise your brain with crossword puzzles and memory games.
6. If you are depressed, get treated.

This is all good information! But it's only good if you use it. This information came from two different public sources. Notice how they reinforce each other a lot. This is good.

Margaret Valone

Thank You All

This is going to be a thank you letter. I owe so much to so many people. I could start at the beginning where my family gave me such a good start or I could start with the present. Earlier this month I spent 10 days in the hospital. I met so many nice people. Some of them recognized me from this column. They were so encouraging. They told me how they waited every week for the column. It makes them laugh and it makes them think They became aware of how much they have and they want to use all the things open to them wisely.

You have no idea how good that makes me feel because I value wisdom so much. And then when that moves people to action, I can hardly contain myself because I'm a person of action. I fill out opinion forms, I write letters to representatives. I make telephone calls, etc. Do I make a difference? I don't know. My duty is to contact people. Their reaction is their responsibility. I can't fix something I don't know is broken or needs to be changed so it's my duty to contact people in places of authority to tell them what I see. Am I going to change the world? Hardly, but I can improve local situations. So can you.

We have the freedom of speaking out. That freedom came with a price. It has great value. Oh, we don't have to be nasty about our observations. As a matter of fact we should be tactful about our observations and offer to help with solutions to the problem. I want to thank Observer publisher John D'Agostino for the freedom he gives me with my column. He never tells me what I can say or how to say it. I have a multitude of interests and I can go all over the place.

The Soup of Life

The first week I was home, a woman called me up and left a message. She loved my column and said, "Thank you, thank you" about 10 times. I don't know her although she identified herself and I want to thank her for taking the time to call.

One woman said to me, "I thought you were Margaret Valone, but she's much taller than you."

I laughed. Every time I had an operation I shrunk, and then there's old age. C'est la vie!

I've talked about freedom which is so valuable, but there's one thing much more precious, and that's love. There are so many kinds of love. I'm not a kissy-kissy person, but I'm a hugger. But we can really show our loving natures by doing things for others. Love in action is fantastic.

For example, I had enough food for a weekend: it was all delicious. As a matter of fact I got spoiled. I had people shop for me, clear my porch, give me rides to church, etc. The boys upstairs are great. One of them brought down a piece of his birthday cake and said to me, "If you need anything, just call. I love to do things for people." I was so glad because I have a helping hand, but I was happier for him. He has learned the joy of doing for others. You can't give without receiving.

If we are smart we will teach those around us the joy of using our loving natures and freedoms.

So many times readers will tell me they can see by my stories that I grew up in a loving home. I thought everybody did. But if you didn't, make sure your own home is easy-going and loving. And Russ's family was just like mine and I love every one of them. If you're already married, show respect for one another and if you're not already married, look for a mate you can respect and shows you respect. Everything else will follow. Teach this to your children. I wish the schools, churches, and the families would all promote the character of respect.

You, readers, have showed me respect, and I thank you.

Margaret Valone

ABOUT THE AUTHOR

I started writing a column over ten years ago. My purpose was that I wanted the readers to have more love, more laughter, and certainly more wisdom. So many readers have told me that the column was the highlight of their week. I was amazed at the men who have responded to the column too.

I am 88 years old and still very involved in life and all the things around me. I believe each of us has a responsibility to grow wise and respond to the world around us. I believe living is a lot more than just breathing! Get involved and make a difference.

My family is working with me to put this book together.

I'm going to start this book with information I have learned that has enriched my life. I hope you love to think. It's so rewarding.

I also did stand-up comedy when I was young because I love to make people laugh. I regret should have done more.

I have named the book "The Soup of Life". Just as the taste of your soup depends upon what you put into it, the quality of your life depends on what you put into it. The good news is that you are in control of your choices. Go for it! The more you put into your life, the more you get out of it. Bon appétit.

This is a common sense book. We all need it. Enjoy! It will make a wonderful gift for those of all ages, male and female. Men like it because truth is truth for all forever.

Made in the USA
Lexington, KY
21 December 2015